U.S.–INDIA RELATIONS: DEMOCRATIC PARTNERS OF ECONOMIC OPPORTUNITY

HEARING

BEFORE THE

SUBCOMMITTEE ON ASIA AND THE PACIFIC

OF THE

COMMITTEE ON FOREIGN AFFAIRS
HOUSE OF REPRESENTATIVES

ONE HUNDRED FOURTEENTH CONGRESS

SECOND SESSION

MARCH 15, 2016

Serial No. 114–159

Printed for the use of the Committee on Foreign Affairs

Available via the World Wide Web: http://www.foreignaffairs.house.gov/ or
http://www.gpo.gov/fdsys/

U.S. GOVERNMENT PUBLISHING OFFICE

99–469PDF   WASHINGTON : 2016

For sale by the Superintendent of Documents, U.S. Government Publishing Office
Internet: bookstore.gpo.gov   Phone: toll free (866) 512–1800; DC area (202) 512–1800
Fax: (202) 512–2104   Mail: Stop IDCC, Washington, DC 20402–0001

CONTENTS

Page

WITNESSES

Alyssa Ayres, Ph.D., senior fellow for India, Pakistan, and South Asia, Council on Foreign Relations 5
Mr. Sadanand Dhume, resident fellow, American Enterprise Institute 18
Mr. Richard M. Rossow, senior fellow and Wadhwani Chair in U.S.-India Policy Studies, Center for Strategic and International Studies 28

LETTERS, STATEMENTS, ETC., SUBMITTED FOR THE HEARING

Alyssa Ayres, Ph.D.: Prepared statement 8
Mr. Sadanand Dhume: Prepared statement 20
Mr. Richard M. Rossow: Prepared statement 31

APPENDIX

Hearing notice 48
Hearing minutes 49
Alyssa Ayres, Ph.D.: Material submitted for the record 50

U.S.–INDIA RELATIONS: DEMOCRATIC PARTNERS OF ECONOMIC OPPORTUNITY

TUESDAY, MARCH 15, 2016

House of Representatives,
Subcommittee on Asia and the Pacific,
Committee on Foreign Affairs,
Washington, DC.

The subcommittee met, pursuant to notice, at 2 o'clock p.m., in room 2172 Rayburn House Office Building, Hon. Matt Salmon (chairman of the subcommittee) presiding.

Mr. Salmon [presiding]. The subcommittee will come to order.

Members present will be permitted to submit written statements to be included in the official hearing record. Without objection, the hearing record will remain open for 5 calendar days to allow statements, questions, and extraneous materials for the record, subject to the length limitation and the rules.

The U.S.-India relationship can be characterized simply as one of enormous potential. It is in the interest of this subcommittee and the United States to see democratic societies prosper, and it is because of this view that India is a natural partner for the United States. The 1.3-billion-person nation has become the focus of U.S. trade and business opportunity. People-to-people connections between the two countries undergrid and bolster this relationship.

As a growing military power, India is also a critical global security partner with the potential to help avert military confrontation and conflict in the Indo-Pacific region. Indeed, both the United States and India recognize the potential partnerships between the world's fastest-growing large economy and the world's most powerful economy.

In light of this, we should expect that bilateral trade has much more room to grow. We convene this hearing today to discuss the U.S.-India economic relationship. Trade in goods and services has ballooned between 2005 and 2015. Both countries have prioritized the economic relationship, aiming to reach $500 billion in bilateral trade in goods and services by 2024, a fivefold increase from the 2014 level.

To achieve this, it is greatly important that India continue substantive economic reform by opening its markets, but substantive challenges remain, including speculation about India's domestic growth products, prospects, limits to market accessibility, and concerns about intellectual property rights protection.

When Prime Minister Modi came into power in 2014, he shouldered high expectations for an economic transformation. While his leadership continues to hold the promise of a new economic era for India, observers have become frustrated with the slow pace of reform. India's economic growth rate at 7.6 percent will not be enough to generate sufficient jobs for India's exploding population of young people.

On top of that, these issues are exacerbated by an overbearing and corrupt bureaucracy, insufficient infrastructure development, heavy regulation, and high social spending. Meaningful reform has been hindered by domestic policies and parliamentary gridlock.

A critical component of India's economic reform will be its involvement in multilateral economic institutions. India has for 20 years shown an interest in joining the Asia-Pacific Economic Cooperation, or APEC, a regional organization that supports economic growth through free and open trade and investment, promoting regional integration and encouraging economic cooperation, among other things.

This has been an ambition that our Executive Branch has welcomed and encouraged. To assist in accelerating the relationship toward this goal, I plan on introducing a bill to support India's membership in APEC this week. Thanks to my colleague Mr. Bera, who has been working with me on putting this bill together.

Our two countries are also in the midst of discussions on a high-standards Bilateral Investment Treaty, or BIT. If achievable, the BIT would deepen our economic relationship and support economic growth and job creation in both countries.

These sorts of positive currents and potential achievements for Indian economic policy would illustrate a movement toward greater openness and harmonization with global free market principles that will be beneficial to India and the U.S.-India relationship and both of our economies.

Such reforms would pave the way to the accelerated growth India needs, and the increased openness would allow our countries to exploit our comparative advantages. Experts estimate that a successful BIT agreement, for example, could increase U.S. goods exports to India by 50 percent or more and could double service exports. A successful BIT could even pave the way forward toward a free trade agreement with India.

Despite the slow pace of reform, India's economy remains a bright spot amidst global economic troubles, particularly for developing nations. It is still the world's fastest-growing large economy, and I look forward to hearing about the U.S.-India economic relationship and the opportunities and challenges that encompass it, and how the United States can best support and nurture the bilateral economic relationship.

I would like to recognize Mr. Sherman for any opening statement he would like to have.

Mr. SHERMAN. Thank you, Mr. Chairman. Thank you for holding this important hearing.

With a population of 1¼ billion people, India is the world's largest democracy, the largest democracy in history. Some 550 million people voted in the last nationwide elections.

When you look at the people of India, you see that many have moved outside India to create a diaspora. Everywhere in the world that diaspora is considerably more educated and considerably wealthier than the country in which it is located. In fact, the only place you can go to find a poor person of Indian heritage is India. I am confident that, as India gets better governance, it will emerge as one of the richer countries in the world.

The United States and India share many core values, including religious pluralism, individual freedom, the rule of law, and electoral democracy, and both have rejected and are working together against radical Islamic extremism. The Indo-American community in the United States is a vital link between the two countries and has helped build bridges. New Delhi has played an important role in regional peace and security. Its growing economic power adds to its ability to deal with strategic issues.

India's growth path shows that it can be compared to China. I used to be a business advisor and now and then give free business advice to those of my constituents foolish enough to ask me for it, and I pointed out that an investment in India makes a lot more sense than one in China. In India you have the rule of law. In India you also have the long-term stability, messy as it is, of governing institutions.

The United States during the Great Depression showed that democracy can survive a 20-, 30-, even 40-percent decline in GDP. I do not think that a system of government built around a party that got power by claiming to be the vanguard of the proletariat, but now says it is not, could survive even zero-percent economic growth for a year or two. So, while China gives this image of stability, it does not have a system which could explain to its people why certain individuals hold positions of power.

Over the past decades, we have seen the U.S. work to bring India out from nuclear isolation and, of course, increase defense and security cooperation. The International Energy Administration estimates that India will require $2.1 trillion of investment in its power sector. Of course, India is looking to develop its own oil and natural gas resources and is seeking $25 billion of investment there. I want to do everything possible to make sure that the tremendous amount of equipment that is necessary for this power expansion is produced in America by American workers.

I was one of 83 Members of Congress, along with at least several people in this room, to urge that this House provide Prime Minister Modi with the highest honor we can provide a foreign leader, and that is an invitation to address a Joint Session of Congress. While the schedule couldn't be worked out last time, I look forward to hearing Prime Minister Modi while sitting on the House Floor.

We look forward to expanding our trade relationship, which is now at only $110 billion. I believe the Vice President and others have announced the goal of expanding that to $500 billion of bilateral trade.

But I will point out that this has got to be balanced trade, that the people of this country have, in case we haven't noticed, risen to totally repudiate the trade policies that we have followed so far, which are misnamed ''free trade.'' Every single Presidential candidate with over 150 delegates has absolutely repudiated the trade policy that has guided us over the last 20 years. Now some of them have done it rather reluctantly, but all of those who are still significant candidates have done so.

So, the people of this country look forward to expanding trade around the world on a balanced basis, not with the United States running huge trade deficits. It will take a completely different model of trade to achieve that. Those who come to the American people and just say all trade is good, no matter whether it is balanced or not, will be, have been utterly repudiated by the people of this country.

And I yield back.

Mr. SALMON. Thank you.

Mr. Bera, did you care to make an opening statement?

Mr. BERA. Sure. Thank you, Mr. Chairman and the ranking member.

I had a chance to travel to India with the chairman of the subcommittee as well as the chairman of the full committee last year and, then, recently returned to India a few months ago. And you still feel the sense of optimism in India, the sense that the economy, while it is not a straight shot, is still quite vigorous and vibrant.

I think the chairman's leadership on the resolution that we will be introducing this week to really encourage India's joining of APEC, that probably is the next logical step as they undergo the economic reforms and undergo much of the agenda that Prime Minister Modi has put out there.

For us to realize this potential that both the President and Vice President have said of creating the defining relationship in the 21st century and trying to take the bilateral trade from $100 billion to $500 billion, you know, APEC membership is a good next step. It will take us a little bit longer to get that high-standard Bilateral Investment Treaty, but that certainly is an aspirational goal for both countries and really can set the framework for bilateral trade.

Now, on our side, I urge patience. The economic reforms in India will take time. I think we have to look at this longer time horizon. On the Indian side, we encourage the Prime Minister to continue the economic reforms to ease the ability of our companies to do business, to put in good intellectual property and patent protections that don't hinder that investment and, also, to open up and ease the ability for U.S. resources and U.S. venture to help India realize its potential. I mean, these are all achievable goals. It requires patience on both sides of the Pacific. It requires open dialog. I remain very optimistic that we can reach those goals.

I look forward to hearing the testimony of witnesses who are all experts on this relationship.

Again, I will yield back.

Mr. SALMON. Thank you.

Ms. Meng, did you have an opening statement?

Ms. MENG. Thank you, Mr. Chairman and to our ranking member.

Thank you to our witnesses who are here today to testify on U.S.-India relations. I represent one of the largest Indian-American diasporas in Congress.

The people-to-people relationship has been a driving force behind bringing our countries closer together. Under this President, our countries have grown closer and we share renewed commitment to working together, particularly in the economic sphere. Principles of our joint commitment were laid out first in September 2014, when U.S. and Indian leaders committed to expanding and deepening the strategic partnership in a vision statement entitled ''Chalein Saath Saath: Forward Together We Go.'' Following President Obama's second state visit to India in January 2015, we released a joint statement outlining extensive, detailed commitment in a variety of industries.

But, while it is clear that there is a deep interest and commitment on both sides, there is still a lot of groundwork we must do to realize this vision. I look forward to hearing from you on how you see the status of this commitment from India and how we can best address some of the existing challenges.

Thank you, and I yield back.

Mr. SALMON. Thank you.

Mr. Lowenthal?

Mr. LOWENTHAL. Thank you, Mr. Chairman.

And thank you, witnesses, for joining us today.

Sitting on this committee, I realize just what an increasingly-complex world in which we live, but how interdependent we are with our global neighbors, how we look forward to working to promote peace, security, economic growth, development.

With India especially, representing such a huge population, proportion of the world's population, I want to know how we can both influence and effectively advance both our national interest and at the same time do that in a way that improves our relationships. You know, there are many challenges in front of us in the world, on this globe, and this committee sees them all. But I want to hear how we can in this committee and Congress support better relationships with India, how we can support their economic development, their democratic aspirations, and not just of India, but really the democratic aspirations of the entire region and how we can work together for that.

And I yield back.

Mr. SALMON. Thank you very much.

We are very fortunate today to be joined by three very distinguished panelists.

First, Alyssa Ayres, Ph.D., senior fellow for India, Pakistan, South Asia, at the Council on Foreign Relations. Welcome, Dr. Ayres.

Mr. Sadanand Dhume, resident fellow at the American Enterprise Institute, and Mr. Richard M. Rossow, senior fellow and Wadhwani Chair in U.S.-India Policy Studies at the Center for Strategic and International Studies.

We will begin with you, Dr. Ayres.

STATEMENT OF ALYSSA AYRES, PH.D., SENIOR FELLOW FOR INDIA, PAKISTAN, AND SOUTH ASIA, COUNCIL ON FOREIGN RELATIONS

Ms. AYRES. Chairman Salmon, Ranking Member Sherman, and members of the subcommittee, thank you very much for the invitation to appear before you today on U.S. economic ties with India. I am honored to be part of this distinguished panel.

I shared in advance with the committee a recent Council on Foreign Relations Independent Task Force report for which I served as project director. I respectfully request that the report and my more detailed written statement be submitted for the record.

In the last 15 years, India has experienced significant economic growth, and the bilateral economic relationship has changed substantially. After several years hovering below the $100-billion level, in 2014 two-way trade in goods and services crossed that threshold and last year reached $107 billion. U.S. exports to India now support more than 180,000 American jobs, as Secretary of Commerce Penny Pritzker said last year.

U.S.-India defense trade has increased from zero to around $13 billion cumulatively. Technology and entrepreneurship are increasingly a bridge between both countries. At the same time, U.S.-India trade remains well below its potential, only a little more than one-tenth U.S.-China trade in goods and more on the scale of Taiwan or the Netherlands.

India and the United States also have market access differences. I do not intend to minimize these concerns, for they certainly exist, but I will focus my remarks on the future strategic horizon we should bear in mind, India's future potential.

According to International Monetary Fund data, India's GDP crossed the $2-trillion threshold in 2014. At market exchange rates, India was the world's ninth largest economy that year, surpassing Russia. India is now growing at around 7.3 percent annually, which in 2015 made India the fastest-growing major economy in the world, given China's slowdown.

India, as you know, does not fare as well when looking at per-capita GDP. When looking at per capita at market exchange rates, India's nearly $1700 level ranks it in the bottom third. Still, the prospect for India's middle class to grow substantially in the coming decades is not in doubt. A strong economic base will allow India to continue on its path of rising global power, including by enabling its military modernization, making the country a bulwark of democracy and stability in an expanded region from the Middle East to East Asia, where both are not always in ample supply.

I referred to the Council on Foreign Relations Independent Task Force. One of its top findings was that, if India can maintain its current growth rate, let alone attain sustained double digits, it has the potential over the next 20 to 30 years to follow China on the path to becoming another $10-trillion economy. Few countries have such potential.

India has its own political work to do to realize these ambitions and it will not be easy. These are challenges that the United States can do little about, but we have a clear stake in India achieving its ambitions.

The Task Force recommended that the United States elevate support for India's economic growth and its reform process to the highest bilateral priority. I will provide several recommendations for how to do this at the end of my testimony.

Preparing the United States for a more global India. We have a problem of underinvestment and insufficient attention to India in United States higher education, an economic preparedness issue for our own country. The ranking of top study-abroad destinations tells an obvious story about American interest in Europe, but China has overtaken Germany as a destination. Nearly twice as many American students head to Costa Rica for an experience abroad than to India.

Language enrollment data is yet more dispiriting. Students in U.S. colleges and universities do not sign up for Indian languages at the levels they do for languages like Arabic, Chinese, or Korean. Here is an example: Enrollments for Hindi were only 1800. All Indian languages combined were around 3,000. This means that the total enrollments in all Indian languages combined account for less than one-quarter those of Korean.

Let me offer now a few recommendations for U.S. policy on these issues. First, elevate support for India's economic growth to the highest bilateral priority on the U.S. agenda with India. Steps recommended by the CFR-sponsored Independent Task Force report include leadership of a global diplomatic effort to support India's entry into APEC; completion of a Bilateral Investment Treaty; high-level discussion of bilateral sectoral agreements such as in services; identification of a longer-term pathway to a free trade agreement or Indian membership in an expanded TPP as an equivalent; creation of initiatives that respond to Indian interest in domestic reform needs such as technical advice on infrastructure finance, and continued emphasis on defense trade and technology.

Second, as India becomes an increasingly-central global economy, the United States should work to integrate India in global economic institutions. I mentioned APEC. There are other institutions in which India should become a member, such as the OECD and the International Energy Agency.

Finally, prepare our next generation for an India in the global economy. Review Federal funding incentives to encourage study abroad in India and study of Indian languages.

Thank you very much, and I look forward to questions.

[The prepared statement of Ms. Ayres follows:]

COUNCIL on FOREIGN RELATIONS

March 15, 2015

Economic Relations With India

Prepared statement by

Alyssa Ayres
Senior Fellow for India, Pakistan, and South Asia
Council on Foreign Relations

Before the

Committee on Foreign Affairs, Subcommittee on Asia and the Pacific
United States House of Representatives
2nd Session, 114th Congress

Hearing on "U.S.-India Relations: Democratic Partners of Economic Opportunity"

Chairman Salmon, Ranking Member Sherman, and Members of the Subcommittee,

Thank you very much for the invitation to appear before you on U.S. economic ties with India. I am honored to be part of this distinguished panel. I shared in advance with the committee a recent Council on Foreign Relations (CFR) Independent Task Force report, for which I served as project director, that addresses many of the issues you wish to explore in some detail. I respectfully request that the report be submitted for the record. My testimony here draws extensively from the Task Force report's findings and recommendations.

U.S.-India ties have been transformed over the past fifteen years, from what was termed for many years a relationship of "estrangement," to one of strategic partnership. From our vantage point today, it is hard to remember what things were like even fifteen years ago, but among the most important differences was a very limited economic relationship. In the intervening years, India has experienced significant economic growth, U.S. businesses have increasingly seen India as an important part of their global strategies, and Indian businesses have increasingly looked to the United States as an investment destination and a market for their services. The large and growing Indian American community, now numbering nearly three million, in recent years has reached the peaks of leadership in American companies, in elected office, in academia, and in so many other fields. The result of these developments has been a stronger support base across both countries for deepening ties.

The bilateral economic relationship has changed substantially. Many will remember former U.S. ambassador to India Robert D. Blackwill's comment in 2002 that U.S.-India trade was "flat as a chapati." I am happy to report it is no longer so flat. After several years hovering below the $100 billion level, in 2014 two-way trade in goods and services crossed that threshold, and last year reached $107 billion. The table below illustrates how two-way goods and services trade grew five-fold in the years from 2002 to 2014.

U.S.-India Two-Way Trade in Goods and Services, 2002–2014			
Year	_Two-way trade in goods_	_Two-way trade in services_	_Overall two-way trade_
2002	$15,967	$5,035	$21,002
2003	$18,131	$5,799	$23,930
2004	$21,795	$7,125	$28,920
2005	$26,910	$9,970	$36,880
2006	$31,744	$13,600	$45,344
2007	$39,281	$18,603	$57,884
2008	$43,732	$22,697	$66,429
2009	$37,816	$22,199	$60,015
2010	$49,016	$25,033	$74,049
2011	$57,994	$29,156	$87,150
2012	$62,948	$31,081	$94,029
2013	$64,174	$32,917	$97,091
2014	$67,935	$35,992	$103,927
2015	$66,660	$40,934	$107,594

Source: U.S. Department of Commerce, Census Bureau, www.census.gov, and Bureau of Economic Analysis, www.bea.gov, March 4, 2016 update.

These growing commercial ties have drawn New Delhi and Washington closer together. In a speech last September, Secretary of Commerce Penny Pritzker noted that U.S. exports to India now "support more than 180,000 American jobs, and India's exports to our country support roughly 365,000 Indian jobs. U.S. firms employ about 840,000 people in India, while Indian-owned companies employ nearly 44,000 people in our communities."[1] This level of economic embeddedness is new, and beneficial to both countries. The U.S.-India Business Council has seen a significant uptick in its membership, now around 450 companies.

---

[1] Secretary of Commerce Penny Pritzker, "U.S. Secretary of Commerce Penny Pritzker Addresses U.S.-India Commercial and Economic Relationship at Carnegie Endowment for International Peace," September 21, 2015.

2

U.S.-India defense trade has increased from approximately zero to around $13 billion in the past decade.[2] U.S. technology industries have strong links with India, and entrepreneurship is increasingly a bridge between both countries. It is no accident that Indian Prime Minister Narendra Modi spent time during his second visit to the United States last September in Silicon Valley, speaking to a group of tech entrepreneurs at the launch of a private-sector "India-U.S. Startup Konnect" initiative.

At the same time, U.S.-India trade remains well below its potential—only a little more than one-tenth of U.S.-China trade in goods, and more on the scale of Taiwan or the Netherlands. Given India's population and the potential size of its economy, a more ambitious target for trade between both countries should be the goal. The Obama administration has held out a target of $500 billion for two-way U.S.-India trade as a vision statement, but the anticipated timeframe as well as the path to get there remains unelaborated. India and the United States also have differences over market access concerns; the United States recently received favorable decisions in two different disputes with India filed in the World Trade Organization (WTO), and India requested consultations with the United States in the WTO over visa issues for highly skilled workers. I do not intend to minimize these concerns, for they certainly exist, but I will focus my remarks on the future potential for this economic relationship in the longer term, as that is the strategic horizon we should bear in mind.

India's Future Potential

According to International Monetary Fund (IMF) data, the Indian economy crossed the $2 trillion threshold in 2014, using market exchange rates to measure gross domestic product (GDP). India is now among the top ten global economies. At market exchange rates, India was the world's ninth largest economy in 2014, surpassing Russia. When using purchasing power parity (PPP) terms, a means of adjusting for the costs within economies to better compare them, India is the world's third largest economy, surpassing Japan. India's economic growth has come back from a dip during the 2011 to 2014 period, and is now growing at around 7.3 percent, which in 2015 made India the fastest-growing major economy in the world given China's slowdown. India's finance ministry declared its ambition to see the country's economy reach $5 trillion (again, at market exchange rates) by 2025.

The IMF estimates that India should see economic growth rates of around 7.5 percent out through 2020. As growth slows in other economies, this lifts India up relative to others. Using IMF staff estimates for the size of global economies in 2015, even using market exchange rates India moves up from the 2014 ranking to surpass Italy and Brazil, becoming the seventh largest economy in the world. This trend matters.

---

[2] Indian Ambassador to the United States Arun K. Singh, "India and U.S.: Shaping a Partnership of the 21st Century," Speech at the University of Michigan, October 14, 2015.

3

Ten Largest Global Economies, GDP (current prices), 2014 data in USD billions		
Rank	Country	2014
1	United States	17,348.08
2	China	10,356.51
3	Japan	4,602.37
4	Germany	3,874.44
5	United Kingdom	2,950.04
6	France	2,833.69
7	Brazil	2,346.58
8	Italy	2,147.74
9	India	2,051.23
10	Russia	1,860.60

Source: International Monetary Fund World Economic Outlook Database, October 2015.

Ten Largest Global Economies, GDP (PPP), 2014 data in USD billions		
Rank	Country	2014
1	China	18,088.05
2	United States	17,348.08
3	India	7,411.09
4	Japan	4,767.16
5	Germany	3,748.09
6	Russia	3,576.84
7	Brazil	3,275.80
8	Indonesia	2,685.89
9	France	2,591.17
10	United Kingdom	2,569.22

Source: International Monetary Fund World Economic Outlook Database, October 2015.

IMF Staff Estimates: Ten Largest Global Economies, GDP (current prices), 2015 data in USD billions		
Rank	Country	2015 est.
1	United States	17,968.20
2	China	11,384.76
3	Japan	4,116.24
4	Germany	3,371.00
5	United Kingdom	2,864.90
6	France	2,422.65
7	India	2,182.58
8	Italy	1,819.05
9	Brazil	1,799.61
10	Canada	1,572.78

Source: International Monetary Fund World Economic Outlook Database, October 2015.

India does not fare as well when looking at per capita GDP, however, reflecting the fact that the country remains home to hundreds of millions of poor. When looking at per capita income at market exchange rates, India's $1,688 level ranks it at number 140 in the world, in the bottom third. Still, economic growth has lifted an estimated 133 million people out of extreme poverty and into low-income status over the 2001 to 2011 period.[3] While estimates vary on the size of India's middle class, from a high of more than half a billion by 2025 in one study, to a low of a little more than thirty million people in another, the prospect for India's middle class to grow substantially in the coming decades is not in doubt.[4] Indian leaders ideally would like to see higher growth rates in the 8 to 10 percent range to generate sufficient jobs for the country's fast-growing workforce age population, to reduce poverty, and to establish India firmly as a global economic leader. A strong economic base will allow India to continue on its path of rising global power, including by enabling its military modernization, making the country a bulwark of democracy and stability in an extended region from the Middle East to East Asia where both are not always in ample supply.

During the latter half of 2015, CFR sponsored an Independent Task Force on U.S.-India relations. One of

---

[3] Rakesh Kochhar, "A Global Middle Class Is More Promise Than Reality: From 2001 to 2011, Nearly 700 Million Step Out of Poverty, but Most Only Barely," Pew Research Center, July 2015.

[4] See Jonathan Ablett et al., "The 'Bird of Gold': The Rise of India's Consumer Market," McKinsey Global Institute, May 2007; Asian Development Bank, "Special Chapter: The Rise of Asia's Middle Class" in Key Indicators for Asia and the Pacific 2010, (Mandaluyong City, Philippines: Asia Development Bank, 2010); Christian Meyer and Nancy Birdsall, "New Estimates of India's Middle Class: Technical Note," Center for Global Development, November 2012; Kochhar, "A Global Middle Class Is More Promise Than Reality."

the Task Force's findings, based on India's economic performance, its potential, and its ambitions, was that **"if India can maintain its current growth rate, let alone attain sustained double digits, it has the potential over the next twenty to thirty years to follow China on the path to becoming another $10 trillion economy."** Few countries have such potential. Our Task Force further noted that "**This places India at a unique moment in which the right choices could propel it to far greater relevance for global GDP growth in the decades to come. Consequently, nothing is more important to India's future success—across all facets of national power—than achieving sustained high levels of annual economic growth.**"[5]

India has its own political work to do to realize these ambitions. It will need to continue economic reforms to meet the sustained high growth rates the country needs to achieve a true transformation of the economy. It will need to keep opening itself further to the world, increase its global trade, make it easier to do business, develop a more significant manufacturing sector, and build a twenty-first century infrastructure that will facilitate increased commerce. None of this will be easy. An effort to reform labor laws, for example, widely seen as so onerous as to have prevented the development of large-scale manufacturing, does not have sufficient political support to pass in parliament, so the government has devolved labor law reform down to individual states. An effort to forge a national goods and services tax has been stymied in at least three sessions of parliament due to opposition protests over unrelated issues. These two examples show how difficult it is even for a government committed in principle to economic reform to gain the political support to do so.

The domestic political challenges to economic reform in India are challenges that the United States can do little about. These are choices for Indian citizens and their elected representatives to make. But we have a clear stake in India achieving its ambitions. As our Task Force observed, "**As the Indian economy grows, it has the potential to become increasingly indispensable for global prosperity—becoming an engine of growth for its region and its trading partners, and rising as a source of global investment.**"[6]

Indeed, just looking at the comparative IMF data over the decades illustrates precisely what this means. In PPP terms, India accounted for a little more than 3 percent of the world total GDP in 1985. That grew to 3.8 percent by 1995, and 4.8 percent by 2005. For 2015, the IMF estimates that India accounted for more than 7 percent of the world total GDP. India's rising share illustrates the global pattern of emerging markets becoming an increasingly larger part of the world economy as they grow. Over time, if the Indian economy continues to grow fast, it will be a vital global economic force.

---

[5] Charles R. Kaye, Joseph S. Nye, Jr., and Alyssa Ayres, "Working With a Rising India: A Joint Venture for the New Century." Independent Task Force Report No. 73 (New York: Council on Foreign Relations Press, November 2015), 11, http://i.cfr.org/content/publications/attachments/TFR73_India.pdf.
[6] Ibid., 15.

Ten Largest Global Economies, GDP (PPP) Share of World Total (%)								
2015 Rank	Country	1985	1990	1995	2000	2005	2010	2015*
1	China	3.408	4.149	5.974	7.498	9.858	13.959	17.241
2	United States	22.629	22.247	20.400	20.928	19.578	16.905	15.878
3	India	3.335	3.712	3.838	4.275	4.895	6.007	7.093
4	Japan	8.252	8.779	7.601	6.586	5.769	4.880	4.279
5	Germany	6.166	6.088	5.413	4.946	4.194	3.705	3.395
6	Russia	n/a	n/a	3.462	3.115	3.460	3.424	3.070
7	Brazil	4.055	3.735	3.490	3.226	3.066	3.167	2.835
8	Indonesia	1.587	1.922	2.262	1.950	2.028	2.264	2.508
9	United Kingdom	3.678	3.646	3.195	3.098	2.955	2.523	2.350
10	France	4.204	4.139	3.560	3.415	3.060	2.644	2.339

* estimates   Source: International Monetary Fund World Economic Outlook Database, October 2015

Given the above observations about India's fast-growing importance to the world economy in the aggregate, and to the U.S. economy as our specific national interest, the Task Force recommended that the United States **"elevate support for India's economic growth and its reform process to the highest bilateral priority, committing to ambitious targets for bilateral economic ties along with clear steps to get there."**[7] I provide specific steps toward this goal drawn from our Task Force report, with some additional recommendations, in the "Recommendations for U.S. Policy" section below.

Among the most important, and one immediately actionable, is for the United States to take action and champion Indian membership in the Asia-Pacific Economic Cooperation (APEC) forum. India seeks membership and has been waiting for nearly twenty years. APEC membership would be a helpful step toward the possibility of considering Indian participation in an expanded Trans-Pacific Partnership (TPP) down the line, and APEC membership would include India in a range of peer consultations committed toward the shared goals of free and open trade and investment. APEC is not a binding negotiating forum, but rather a norm-setting organization with a commitment to transparency and continued work to further open trade goals. India would benefit from inclusion in ongoing consultation with Asia-Pacific peers on how the economic region can further trade.[8]

In January 2015, during his visit to India for Republic Day, President Barack Obama issued a joint vision statement with Prime Minister Modi on cooperation in the Asia Pacific and Indian Ocean; the vision statement noted that the United States "welcomes India's interest in joining the Asia Pacific Economic

---

[7] Ibid., 34.

[8] For a longer discussion of India and APEC, see Alyssa Ayres, "Bringing India Inside the Asian Trade Tent," Policy Innovation Memorandum No. 46 (New York: Council on Foreign Relations Press, June 2014), http://www.cfr.org/india/bringing-india-inside-asian-trade-tent/p33173.

Cooperation forum, as the Indian economy is a dynamic part of the Asian economy."[9] In the more than one year since that statement, the United States has taken no action on India's interest in APEC. A commonly expressed concern is that given India's domestic protections in a variety of sectors, and given India's demonstrated tough negotiation postures in the WTO, India may not be "ready" for APEC and may make it more difficult for this consensus-based organization to make decisions. Here, the fact that this is not a binding forum matters; it is a community of shared norms focused on greater openness. India is now Asia's fastest-growing economy and a colossus in its own right; the benefits of including India in this consultative process should outweigh in strategic gains any potential losses to efficiency.

Preparing the United States for a More Global India

Given India's trajectory of increasing prominence in the world and as an important American partner, we ought to prepare our own rising generations for that future. This is an economic preparedness issue for our own country. For nearly fifteen years I have been concerned about the underinvestment and insufficient attention India receives in U.S. higher education. American students do not study abroad in India at the levels one might expect given its role as a rising global power. Americans do not study Indian languages— and admittedly there are many—at the levels they do for Chinese, or even American Sign Language.

The ranking of top study abroad destinations tells an obvious story about the special relationship between the United States and the United Kingdom, but Italy, Spain, and France are not far behind. China has overtaken Germany as a destination. Nearly twice as many American students head to Costa Rica for an experience abroad than to India. Costa Rica is wonderful, but it is not a rising power like India.

Rank	Country	Enrollments
1	United Kingdom	38,250
2	Italy	31,166
3	Spain	26,949
4	France	17,597
5	China	13,763
6	Germany	10,377
7	Ireland	8,823
8	Costa Rica	8,578
9	Australia	8,369
10	Japan	5,978
11	South Africa	4,968
12	India	4,583

Leading Destinations of U.S. Study Abroad Students, 2013–2014

Source: Open Doors data, International Institute of Education, 2015.

---

[9] The White House Office of the Press Secretary. "U.S.-India Joint Strategic Vision for the Asia-Pacific and Indian Ocean Region." January 25, 2015.

Language enrollment data is yet more dispiriting. Students in U.S. colleges and universities do not sign up for Indian languages at the levels they do for languages like Arabic, Chinese, or Korean. Neither geopolitical attention nor India's economic rise spurred interest in Indian languages like Japanese, Chinese, and Korean have seen. India's many languages make it harder to compare with each of these, but even when including all the Indian language enrollments in the United States combined, the number still doesn't cross four thousand. Worse, in 2013 Indian language enrollments *dropped* to 3,090 from the 3,924 of 2009.[10]

Enrollments of Selected Foreign Languages in U.S. Higher Education, 2013			
Language	**Enrollments**	**Language**	**Enrollments**
Spanish	790,756	Latin	27,192
French	197,757	Russian	21,962
American Sign Language	109,577	Ancient Greek	12,917
German	86,700	Biblical Hebrew	12,551
Italian	71,285	Portuguese	12,415
Japanese	66,740	Korean	12,229
Chinese	61,055	Modern Hebrew	6,698
Arabic	32,286	**All Indian languages combined**	**3,090**

Source: Enrollments in Languages Other Than English in United States Institutions of Higher Education, Modern Language Association, 2013.

Enrollments for Hindi—broken out from the aggregate of all Indian languages—were only 1,800. This means that the total enrollments in all Indian languages combined account for <u>less than one-quarter</u> those of Korean, and a mere fraction of more commonly taught languages (14 percent of Russian, 9.5 percent of Arabic, or 5 percent of Chinese).

There are numerous other metrics to illustrate this same general point: that within U.S. higher education, India is not getting the attention that it deserves nor that commensurate with a rising global power. U.S. funding mechanisms through the Higher Education Act routinely prioritize numerous other regions, providing greater resources for East Asia, Latin America, Russia and Eastern Europe, the Middle East, and Africa than for South Asia. The Fulbright mechanism has increased exchange between the United States and India for postgraduate and faculty fellowships, as the Indian government now shares the costs (and indeed, now the name: these are now called Fulbright-Nehru fellowships). But as Americans we ought to review more closely the incentive mechanisms to encourage students during their formative undergraduate years to study abroad in India, study a language, and learn more about this important rising power.

---

[10] Data from the Modern Language Association's enrollments survey database, https://apps.mla.org/flsurvey_search. For the most recent MLA survey report, see David Goldberg, Dennis Looney, and Natalia Lusin, "Enrollments in Languages Other Than English in United States Institutions of Higher Education, Fall 2013," MLA Quadrennial Language Enrollments Survey (New York: Modern Language Association, February 2015).

8

Recommendations for U.S. policy

1. **Elevate support for India's economic growth to the highest bilateral priority for the U.S. agenda with India. Steps recommended by the CFR-sponsored Independent Task Force on U.S.-India Relations include**
   - leadership of a global diplomatic effort to support India's entry into APEC;
   - completion of a bilateral investment treaty;
   - high-level discussion of bilateral sectoral agreements, such as in services;
   - identification of a longer-term pathway to a free trade agreement or Indian membership in an expanded TPP as an equivalent;
   - creation of initiatives that respond to Indian interest in domestic reform needs, such as technical advice on market-based approaches to infrastructure financing; shared work with international financial institutions to reprioritize infrastructure financing; continued joint work on science and technology; technical cooperation on regulatory reform, bank restructuring, best practices in manufacturing, labor, supply chain, transportation, and vocational skills training;
   - continued emphasis on defense trade and technology.[11]

2. **As India becomes an increasingly central global economy, the United States should work more comprehensively to integrate India in global economic institutions.** APEC should be the highest priority, discussed above. There are other economic institutions in which India should become a member. India currently holds "key partner" status in the Organization for Economic Cooperation and Development (OECD), but it should become a member. This is one of the world's primary information-sharing mechanisms on global development, a conversation India has been participating in, but not as a full member. OECD membership would also open up the opportunity for Indian membership in the International Energy Agency (IEA). Again, India is a "key partner" of the IEA, but as India ranks among the world's top energy importers, it no longer makes sense for it to be outside this organization.

3. **Prepare our next generation: Review federal funding incentives to encourage study abroad in India and study of Indian languages.** There are many ways this could be done in addition to the ongoing Higher Education Act funding incentives, which I recognize fall outside of the purview of the House Foreign Affairs Committee.
   - A relatively new initiative, Passport to India, designed to encourage American students to study or participate in service-learning internships in India, has not received the levels of support compared with a similar initiative focused on China, 100,000 Strong. Passport to India is administered by Ohio State University and the State Department.
   - Explore different mechanisms to incentivize study of India and Indian languages. The Boren national security fellowships offer one model, as they incentivize study of less commonly taught

---

[11] Kaye, Nye, Jr., and Ayres, "Working With a Rising India," 35–36.

languages.

- In 1983, Congress created the Title VIII authority to encourage study of Russia and Eastern Europe, administered by the State Department, so therefore offers another model. It is a supplemental authority to the programs supported under the Higher Education Act.

Mr. SALMON. Thank you, Dr. Ayres.
Mr. Dhume?

STATEMENT OF MR. SADANAND DHUME, RESIDENT FELLOW, AMERICAN ENTERPRISE INSTITUTE

Mr. DHUME. Chairman Salmon, Ranking Member Sherman, members of the subcommittee, thank you for this opportunity to testify before the subcommittee on U.S.-India relations, democratic partners of economic opportunity.

I am Sadanand Dhume, resident fellow of the American Enterprise Institute, based here in Washington, DC. My comments today are my own and do not necessarily reflect the views of AEI.

Since our time is limited, I would like to take this opportunity to make four broad points on which I will then elaborate.

Number one, the U.S.-India relationship is a pivotal relationship for the future of the Asia-Pacific and, indeed, the world.

Number two, at a time of political turbulence, it is important for us not to lose sight of the economic principles that have helped make this country the strongest and most prosperous in human history. These include an openness to trade and a welcome mat for talented professionals from around the world.

Number three, after the election of Prime Minister Narendra Modi 2 years ago, India is on the cusp of change. The U.S. cannot determine the policies India will follow, but, by the force of its example and its advocacy, it can nudge India in the direction of the policies that will grow its economy, eradicate poverty, and make it one of America's major global trade partners.

Finally, number four, U.S. economic policy toward India should be tethered to twin goals, to help India achieve its economic potential and to strive to remain India's top trading partner in goods and services.

I will spend the remainder of my time to expanding briefly upon each of these four points.

The first, of course, is that the U.S.-India relationship is pivotal. Sandwiched between a rising China and the turmoil of Afghanistan and Pakistan, India represents an anchor of democratic stability in an uncertain part of the world.

The U.S. stakes in India go beyond economics. But, arguably, no aspect of the relationship is more important than the economic one. Simply put, the U.S. ought to view the goal of making India prosperous in a way similar to which it viewed South Korea, Japan, and Taiwan during the Cold War. This is part of a larger strategic goal which is important to the United States, given what is unfolding in Asia.

In purchasing power priority terms, India is currently the third largest economy, but, as a U.S. trading partner, it is only number 10 in terms of goods trade. I think that gap between those two numbers, number three and number 10, really sums up the challenge that we face, but also the opportunity for further growth.

In terms of India's own potential, though it has had 25 years of rapid growth of about 6 percent a year, in terms of per-capita income it remains at $5,700 a year in purchasing power terms, which is, to put it in perspective, less than half of China. So, again, we have seen quite a dramatic success story over the past 25 years, but there remains a lot of potential for further growth.

I also think that we should keep sight of our larger principles, particularly at a time of turbulence. Arguably, now more than ever, we need to stand by the ideas that have been the bedrock of prosperity for more than 200 years. This means leading by example in terms of openness to trade in both goods and services, while at the same time ceaselessly advocating for greater economic freedom in India. I would like to say, in particular, that some of the debates about Indian tech firms tend to lose sight of the fact that they have been an asset for U.S. competitiveness and Indian tech workers have been productive members of society.

India is on the cusp of change. In 2014, Narendra Modi was elected Prime Minister with India's first single-party majority in 30 years. Mr. Modi earned the reputation as an efficient business-friendly administrator. He has embarked upon reforms, but those reforms have not gone fast enough for many observers. Nonetheless, he is less than 2 years into a 5-year term and he remains the single best bet for India to achieve the economic transformation that it ought to achieve. And it remains in the United States' interest to back him as he makes these efforts.

Finally, to sum up, I would say that all U.S. policy goals, including some of those mentioned by Dr. Ayres, such as backing India's APEC membership, supporting a Bilateral Investment Treaty, I would add to that finding a way to work with India's most dynamic states such as Gujarat and Andhra Pradesh, and also working to enlarge global economic institutions, all of these exist within a larger framework, and that larger framework is two twin ambitions. The first is to help India achieve its economic potential, and the second is to continue to be India's top trade partner in goods and services in the foreseeable future.

Thank you very much.

[The prepared statement of Mr. Dhume follows:]

American Enterprise Institute for Public Policy Research

Statement before the House Committee on Foreign Affairs
Subcommittee on Asia and the Pacific

U.S-India Relations: Democratic Partners of Economic Opportunity

Sadanand Dhume

Resident Fellow

American Enterprise Institute

March 15, 2016

Mr. Chairman, Mr. Ranking Member, thank you for the opportunity to testify today before the Committee on "U.S.-India Relations: Democratic Partners of Economic Opportunity." I am Sadanand Dhume, a resident fellow at the American Enterprise Institute, a non-profit, non-partisan public policy research organization based in Washington, DC. My comments today are my own and do not necessarily reflect the views of AEI.

Over the past two decades, both Democratic and Republican administrations, boosted by bipartisan support in Congress, have recognized the importance of building strong ties with India. The world's most populous democracy occupies a pivotal place in Asia, sandwiched between a rising China and the turmoil of Pakistan and Afghanistan. U.S. hopes for fostering peace and prosperity in Asia rest in no small measure on deepening the U.S.-India relationship.

For the most part, however, economic ties between the two countries have not kept pace with a growing strategic convergence. With an annual output of $2 trillion, India is the ninth largest economy in the world. In purchasing power parity terms it is even larger—a $7.4 trillion economy, or the world's third-largest. Yet, in 2015, India was only the U.S.'s tenth largest trading partner in goods, ranked below smaller economies such as Taiwan and South Korea. Trade in goods amounted to $66.3 billion. Trade in goods and services combined came to $107 billion.

Though India's economy is large in absolute terms, it has so far failed to fully live up to its potential. Per capita income of $5,700 (in PPP terms) is less than half that of China, though both countries had similar levels of per capita income barely 35 years ago. With a median age of 27, India is one of the youngest large countries in the world. In order to provide jobs to the 12 million people who enter the workforce each year, New Delhi will have to significantly deepen an economic reform program first embarked upon 25 years ago, but that has lost steam over the past decade.

The U.S. has an interest in India emerging as a prosperous, market-oriented democracy and a strong American trading partner fully integrated into the global economy. These twin goals should anchor U.S. economic policy toward India.

Key policy recommendations:

- *Asia-Pacific Economic Cooperation:* Back India for full membership in APEC as a step toward eventual inclusion in the Trans-Pacific Partnership.

- *Bilateral Investment Treaty (BIT):* Negotiate a high-quality BIT as a stepping stone toward a free trade agreement.

- *Focus on States:* Recognize a trend towards greater federalism in the Indian economy and deepen relations with the fastest-industrializing states.

- *Champion free market principles:* Instead of focusing solely on specific firms or areas of the economy, the U.S. should broadly support the principles of free enterprise that will allow India to unlock its economic potential.

Background:

India's tryst with socialism. Between independence in 1947 and the advent of economic reforms in 1991, India was one of Asia's worst performing economies. Mistrustful of both free enterprise and trade, India's rulers embraced autarky and state planning. Over time, the country's economy became synonymous with the infamous license-permit raj, where bureaucrats made decisions on factory output, and businessmen needed to worry more about whimsical government officials than about consumers.

In the first three decades after independence (1947-77), despite a low base, the Indian economy grew at an anemic annual average of 3.5 percent. In 1964, the average Indian was about three-fourths as rich as the average South Korean. By 1984, the average South Korean was four times richer than the average Indian.

In 1991, faced with a balance of payments crisis, India finally embarked upon economic reforms. It scrapped industrial licensing, freed imports and exports, slashed trade tariffs, and made room for the private sector in areas once monopolized by government. The economy immediately boomed.

Over the next 13 years, India's reform program deepened, albeit in fits and starts. A new telecom policy led to India's mobile phone revolution. India currently has 1 billion mobile phone subscribers, the second highest number in the world. Competitive private firms have changed the face of Indian telecoms and aviation, and have made deep inroads in banking.

Between 1991 and 2011, the Indian economy grew on average at 6.7 percent per year. However, the reform process lost steam after 2004, when a left-of-center government took power. Though the economy continued to grow—buoyed by healthy global conditions and reforms unfurled before 2004—ultimately the lack of fresh reforms caught up with India. According to the World Bank, growth fell from a high of 10.3 percent in 2010 to 5.1 percent in 2012. By the end of 2013, with the stock market falling and the rupee hitting historic lows against the dollar, India had come to be seen as one of the world's "fragile five" economies.

The rise of Narendra Modi. The election of Narendra Modi as prime minister in 2014, with the first single party electoral majority in 30 years, raised hopes that India would return emphatically to the path of economic reform. On the campaign trail, Modi painted his vision for the economy through slogans such as: "minimum government, maximum governance," "red carpet, not red tape," and "the government has no business being in business."

Modi's record as the dynamic and business-friendly chief minister (the Indian equivalent of governor) of the industrialized western state of Gujarat (2001-14) also raised hopes among many investors and commentators of the kind of far-reaching reforms that had eluded India over the past decade.

So far, the Modi government's record has been mixed. It has done its best to roll out a red carpet for investors, with the prime minister himself acting as India's chief pitchman. Foreign investment norms have been eased in, among other areas, defense, insurance and food processing. Between May 2014 and December 2015, foreign direct investment in India rose 33 percent to $64 billion compared to $48 billion in the 20 months before Modi's election. Several high profile firms, including Taiwan's Foxconn and South Korea's Posco have pledged billions of dollars of fresh investment in India. Large U.S. investors include General Electric, General Motors, Uber and Oracle.

The International Monetary Fund expects India's GDP to grow at 7.5 percent this year, which would make it the world's fastest growing major economy. The government also intends to boost infrastructure spending to $32 billion dollars this year, a 22.5 percent increase from the previous year, in order to upgrade India's roads, ports and railways. Despite stepped-up government spending, Finance Minister Arun Jaitley expects to keep India's fiscal deficit in check at a reasonable 3.5 percent of GDP next year. The government also hopes to end harassment by tax officials by simplifying rules. This is part of a larger effort to improve India's Ease of Doing Business ranking, which despite government efforts to improve it, is currently an unimpressive 130 of 189 countries surveyed by the World Bank.

However, in terms of deep structural reform, the government has either been stymied by the opposition or has itself preferred caution to boldness. Thanks to opposition in the indirectly elected upper house of Parliament, a proposed goods and services tax to stitch India into a common market won't be rolled out this April as planned. The opposition has also forced the government to retreat on a proposal to ease land-acquisition norms for industry.

Labor law reform—in effect making it easier for firms to lay off workers during a downturn—has been shunted to the states, but only a handful of them appear interested in pursuing them seriously. A proposed privatization program has stalled. Though the government says it remains committed to privatization, the prime minister has also suggested that he can stem the rot in state-owned companies simply by picking the right managers.

Despite having a comfortable majority in the lower house of Parliament, the Modi government has done nothing to reverse the previous government's worst laws, like an unpopular retroactive tax. Also in force is a government directive compelling companies to channel some of their profits toward social objectives such as reducing child mortality and combating AIDS. In reality, politicians use the provision to "encourage" businessmen to fund their favorite boondoggles.

Instead of winding up the previous government's flagship make-work program—a notoriously leaky rural job guarantee that wasted billions of dollars—the Modi government has increased its funding to a record level.

Constraints on economic reform. Despite his sweeping electoral victory two years ago, Modi faces massive challenges in pushing a reform agenda. To begin with, the ruling Bharatiya Janata Party (BJP) and its allies control only 63 of 245 seats in the indirectly elected upper house of Parliament. Analysts expect the ruling alliance's numbers to rise to around 72 by the end of the year, but this will still leave it well short of a majority in the upper house.

Moreover, the BJP and its allies only control 11 of India's 29 states. An ambitious devolution program transferring more resources to the states, as well as the rise of powerful regional political parties, ensure that many of the most important economic decisions are made in state capitals, and not in New Delhi.

Despite India's impressive economic gains over the past 25 years, in many ways the country's intellectual and political climate remain hostile to reforms. Modi's BJP has lost two important state elections since February of last year. In both cases, the winning regional party accused Modi of caring more about wealthy businessmen than about the poor. Much of the media too subscribes to the (inaccurate) view that encouraging business and investment signals callousness toward the poor. Similarly, outside of a handful of commentators, there is no obvious constituency in India for free trade.

Finally, though India has been a major beneficiary from lower oil prices—it imports about 80 percent of its oil—uncertainty about the global economy, both a slowing China and a stagnant Europe, have helped put policymakers in New Delhi in a defensive crouch.

What the U.S. can do:

From an economic perspective, the twin goals of the U.S. are straightforward. Washington should continue to encourage the emergence of India as a prosperous and strong democracy that acts as a stabilizing force in the region and beyond. At the same time, the U.S. needs to deepen trade ties with India with the strategic goal of remaining India's largest single trading partner taking into account both goods and services.

In terms of policy options, the U.S. has little ability to influence the economic course India chooses. U.S. officials and business leaders can make the case for economic reforms, but the reason many desired reforms have been spoken of for more than a decade without meaningful progress is that they represent difficult political choices.

Regardless of party affiliation, Indian politicians tend to think twice about rolling back expensive subsidies on food and fertilizer or privatizing loss-making state-owned firms. Such measures cost votes. No foreign country is in a position to nudge Indian policymakers on such sensitive issues. Indeed, even the suggestion of doing so would likely provoke an immediate backlash among sections of India's fiercely nationalistic media.

However, while acknowledging its limited role in influencing the pace of economic reform in India, the U.S. can still strive to both better India's economic prospects and boost commercial ties between the two countries.

Asia-Pacific Economic Cooperation. *Back India for full membership in APEC as a step toward eventual inclusion in the Trans-Pacific Partnership.*

Founded in 1989, the 21-nation APEC is East Asia's broadest economic grouping and the world's largest trading bloc, accounting for three billion consumers and 44 percent of global trade. In 2010, a decade-long moratorium on new members expired, opening the door for India, whose initial application for membership in 1991 was rejected.

The U.S. has welcomed India's interest in joining APEC, but has not backed formal membership. Publicly backing India's candidacy for APEC membership would echo a broad U.S. policy that supports India's rise as a responsible global power. Washington has already supported Indian membership in the G-20, four multilateral nonproliferation regimes, and an expanded United Nations Security Council. In addition, India is already a full member of the East Asian Summit and the ASEAN Regional Forum, and is a dialogue partner with ASEAN.

The case against backing India's entry into APEC hinges on its notoriously obstreperous trade negotiators, who some of their American counterparts hold responsible for helping create a stalemate at the World Trade Organization. They fear that admitting India into APEC will hurt the group's capacity for consensus building and dilute the quality of its trade agreements.

Although these concerns are legitimate, backing India's APEC membership is a low-risk gambit for the United States and carries potentially large rewards. At worst, India complicates the workings of an already unwieldy body that concludes nonbinding agreements among members. At best, India uses APEC membership as training wheels to prepare it for the more ambitious Trans-Pacific Partnership (TPP), embraces the best practices APEC espouses, invigorates the grouping with new energy, and integrates itself more fully into the global economy.

Bilateral Investment Treaty. *Negotiate a high-quality BIT as a stepping stone toward a free trade agreement.*

A U.S.-India BIT will signal renewed purpose in bilateral economic relations, level the playing field for U.S. firms in India, and pave the way for a more ambitious free trade agreement. A BIT with India was first proposed by the George W. Bush administration, but progress on it has long languished in both countries. Both countries support the idea of a U.S.-India investment treaty, but in practice progress toward it has been slow.

Less comprehensive than a free trade agreement, a BIT nonetheless facilitates foreign investment by ensuring so-called national treatment of foreign firms, limiting government expropriation, and providing for binding arbitration between investors and governments. Currently, the U.S. has operational BITs with over 40 countries, including Bangladesh and Sri Lanka in South Asia.

Some supporters of the U.S.-India relationship regard a BIT as trivial given the size of the U.S. and Indian economies, and the scale of ambition a "strategic partnership" between the two countries suggests. This is true, but negotiating a BIT remains a good idea, not as an end in itself but as a significant marker toward the broader—but at this point politically unfeasible—goal of an FTA. A BIT will not by itself transform U.S.-India trade ties, but the inability to negotiate one despite years of trying acts as a damper on the two countries making meaningful progress on trade.

Focus on States. *Recognize a trend towards greater federalism in the Indian economy and deepen relations with the fastest industrializing states.*

As India grows richer and more urban, it is also growing more federal. Last year, the government sharply upped the share of states in federal taxes to 42 percent. As Morgan Stanley's Ruchir Sharma puts it, after a long period of highly centralized rule, India "is rediscovering its natural fabric as a nation of strong regions."

The U.S. should seize the opportunity to focus on India's most entrepreneurial states on the western and southern coasts. U.S. success with federalism, and in building some of the world's greatest cities from scratch, can be particularly helpful to India's fast-urbanizing states. Moreover, the Indian-American diaspora, disproportionately drawn from economically dynamic regions such as Gujarat and Andhra Pradesh, offers a natural bridge toward closer subnational business ties. Reliable estimates are difficult to come by, but on the high side some suggest that about half of Indian-Americans trace their origin to Gujarat.

Devolution in India means powerful state-level satraps will exert greater influence on the federal government in New Delhi and at the same time, carve out more decision-making power for themselves in the country's 29 states, many of which are more populous than most countries. A more federal and urban India will likely show greater entrepreneurial dynamism and produce greater prosperity faster than before. High-performing states also offer India the best opportunity to reform an overly populist political culture that holds the country back. Politicians such as Gujarat's Narendra Modi (as chief minister), Andhra Pradesh's N. Chandrababu Naidu, and Odisha's Naveen Patnaik, have proved that even in India business-friendly leaders can be elected.

Champion free market principles. Instead of focusing solely on specific firms or areas of the economy, the U.S. should broadly support the principles of free enterprise that will allow India to unlock its economic potential.

If economic relations between the U.S. and India are to avoid getting bogged down in minutiae, and are instead to serve U.S. strategic goals in Asia, the U.S. should encourage India to become a more competitive, market-oriented economy for its own sake, even if specific reforms offer no clear payoff for U.S. firms. For instance, India needs better roads, but given the lack of U.S. competitiveness in this area they are unlikely to be built by American firms, though they may at times be built with American equipment.

At the same time, the U.S. should aim to remain India's top trade partner. Last year, Secretary of State John Kerry reiterated the goal of multiplying U.S.–India trade fivefold, to $500 billion, over ten years. But beyond just that number, the U.S. should also aim to stay ahead of China in volume of bilateral trade with India. This will likely spur more day-to-day attention to the relationship than a theoretical longer-term target would.

While consistently advocating for U.S. businesses, Washington should not allow individual companies to hijack the agenda. For instance, while India will undoubtedly benefit from opening up its retail market to Walmart and others, this is not necessarily the most pressing economic issue facing the country.

India needs to liberalize its labor and land markets, rationalize expensive food, fuel, and fertilizer subsidies, and privatize loss-making state-owned companies. Over time, as India's economy becomes bigger and more outward-looking, many of these decisions will likely benefit U.S. companies. But they're important mostly because they will unleash India's own economy, raise the living standards of its people, and give it the wherewithal to fulfil the larger role it seeks on the world stage. Though the U.S. cannot make policy for India, it can certainly provide assistance to would-be Indian reformers who look to it for ideas and expertise.

During the Cold War, the U.S. understood that it had a stake in the economic success of countries as different as South Korea and Indonesia. Today, the future of Asia hinges, to a significant degree, on the evolution of India. If it pays off, America's bet on India could be one of the most important investments it makes in the years ahead.

Mr. SALMON. Thank you.

Mr. Rossow?

STATEMENT OF MR. RICHARD M. ROSSOW, SENIOR FELLOW AND WADHWANI CHAIR IN U.S.–INDIA POLICY STUDIES, CENTER FOR STRATEGIC AND INTERNATIONAL STUDIES

Mr. ROSSOW. Thank you, Chairman Salmon, Ranking Member Sherman, members of the committee. Thank you for the opportunity to testify at this hearing on U.S.-India economic relations.

I will focus my remarks on two main issues that I think must be addressed in order to deepen our economic partnership with India and create new opportunities for American firms. First is that we have to bridge this gap that exists in our approaches to global trade, and the second is we must engage India's regional leaders more directly.

Since Prime Minister Modi took office in 2014, our bilateral relationship has strengthened mightily, though I think in surprising ways, ways that we didn't expect to see. We expected the Modi government to have a strong economic focus, which it has within political limitations. But I think what you could have expected was the establishment of a stronger ideological framework guiding the continued expansion of our strategic partnership. We now have a big disparity, shared security goals that guide that strategic partnership, highlighted I think by the Joint Strategic Vision on Asia-Pacific and the Indian Ocean Region signed last year. But we don't have a similar ideological construct that guides our economic engagement.

Now kind of following on what others have stated before me, but a few examples that highlight the lack of a common ground on global economic issues, today we are no further along than we were 8 years on signing this investment treaty; in fact, a little bit further away, since both the United States and India have amended our model treaties which I think take them further away than they were at the outset.

India is not part of any of the wider trade agreements that the United States is a party of, and a wide chasm remains between our positions on many issues in the World Trade Organization. Now, in truth, I think it is likely that the Indian Government will only begin to approach global trade talks more proactively once their agriculture and manufacturing industries become more globally competitive. The two sectors make up 70 percent of India's workforce, yet contribute only about 45 percent of India's GDP.

But there are a wider range of shared interests. Both countries are hotbeds of innovation. We both have strong services economies. Both have large net trade deficits, particularly with China. We face similar challenges in the way that we have been engaging on global trade issues, and our firms bring complementary to markets like sub-Saharan Africa. I think there is actually a foundation of issues that could create a bit of a more powerful economic narrative on why we should be partners rather than constantly fighting on these big global issues.

The second issue I want to highlight is the importance of developing a more robust whole-of-government strategy to engage India's powerful state regional leaders. State governments—I mean,

I have already heard it a number of times today about Modi reform, has he done enough; has he not done enough?—state governments actually have a much deeper control on India's business environment outside of things like high-level market access than national leaders do. Issues like electricity, water, sanitation, infrastructure, industrial licenses, and law and order, these are all issues that the states actually govern far more than the Federal Government has a hand in.

India's two national parties, Congress and BJP, combined only control 16 of India's 29 states right now. With a few notable exceptions, most of these state leaders actually have very little vision today for what partnership with the United States looks like.

In addition to the strong impact on the local business environment, regional parties in India also have a strong influence on central government policymaking. Regional parties hold the majority of seats in the upper house of India's Parliament.

Also, while we talk about the BJP's electoral victory in the 2014 national election, it is the first time in 30 years that any party won a single-party majority in the lower house of Parliament. We can expect that in the not-too-distant future we will see coalition governments again, and these regional parties played a dramatic influence on policymaking in the last government under coalition governments.

Now taking a step back, I think the Modi government's track record on reforms is somewhat underappreciated. From the U.S. viewpoint, the day that he stepped into office there were four main areas of contention in our economic relationship: Contentious taxation policies; lack of progress on new market access reforms, particularly foreign equity caps; treatment of pharmaceutical patents, and the establishment of forced local content rules in several manufacturing sectors. Those are the four that I saw as really kind of driving the negative sentiments and the hope when Modi stepped into office.

I think 2 years later we have actually seen robust movement on cross-border taxation policies and at the same time dramatic improvement on foreign equity limitations. About 30 sectors have actually seen foreign equity limitations removed or lessened somewhat since he came into office, but we have seen less movement on local content rules in manufacturing and patent laws.

Now these are, of course, the economic agenda as it matters to American firms and policymakers. There are also other reforms that I think haven't been appreciated on this side of the ocean, but in terms of growing the Indian economy and providing new opportunities for American firms would do so. Liberalizing the oil and gas sector; they liberalized the coal sector; transparent auctions for the first time with public resources like spectrum and mining licenses; delicensing defense production of the private sector.

These reforms and India's relatively-high growth rates compared to other countries I think make it an important market to American firms, as has already been stated. Now our economic relationship going forward will benefit from forging a set of shared principles behind global economic issues and for better engagement with India's powerful state leaders.

I was also asked by the committee to offer a couple of recommendations for this committee and for Congress. And so, two things that I have in mind on that.

First, I think the pipeline of congressional visits is terrific, and I think using that kind of an opportunity to engage some of these regional leaders, as what happened with Prime Minister Modi, in fact, before he became the leader of the country, is important to maintain and build on, not just Delhi and Bengal and Bombay, but some of the other regional capitals as well.

Second, we have an election coming up. As I like to joke, you don't become Secretary of State based on your policy toward India. So, we don't really know what the next administration, whoever it is, what their position is going to be on key issues in India. But Congress will still be there, and there is going to be an important role to make sure that we maintain quickly and deeply with India after the election takes place.

So, thank you again for inviting me to appear before the subcommittee.

[The prepared statement of Mr. Rossow follows:]

CSIS | CENTER FOR STRATEGIC &
INTERNATIONAL STUDIES

Statement before the

House Committee on Foreign Affairs

Subcommittee on Asia and the Pacific

"U.S.-India Relations: Democratic Partners of Economic Opportunity"

A Testimony by:

Richard M. Rossow

Senior Fellow,

Wadhwani Chair,

Center for Strategic and International Studies (CSIS)

March 15, 2016

2172 Rayburn House Office Building

WWW.CSIS.ORG | 1616 RHODE ISLAND AVENUE NW | TEL. (202) 887.0700
WASHINGTON, DC 20036 | FAX (202) 775.3199

Chairman Salmon, Ranking Member Sherman,

Thank you for your interest in exploring the state, and future, of our nation's economic relationship with India.

Our relationship with India naturally runs on multiple tracks, which have generally deepened over time. The electoral victory by the Bharatiya Janata Party (BJP) in May 2014 marked a significant turning point in our bilateral relationship. We knew India's Prime Minister, Narendra Modi, would be a strong proponent of economic growth; what few could foresee was his forward-leaning security posture—which is closely aligned with our own. In fact, in the last fourteen months our two countries have reshaped the ideological basis for our security partnership, articulating a wider range of shared interests than ever before—amid growing operational convergences.

However, on the economic front, we have two distinct sets of issues that must be overcome before we can really take advantage of shared economic opportunities. First, our two nations need to forge a set of shared guiding principles for our bilateral and multilateral economic engagement. And second, the United States needs to refocus our engagement strategy to increase the attention we devote to India's state leaders.

The BJP has never been bound by the two Congress Party principles—non-alignment and state-led socialism—that have been ideological constraints on our partnership for most of India's independent history. That does not mean that the BJP is naturally inclined towards a deeper partnership with the United States. But the door is certainly open, as we saw during the last BJP government from 1998-2004. That six year period started with India's nuclear test, and ended with the outline of a roadmap for civilian nuclear cooperation. And the BJP's economic reform program, infrastructure build-out, and embrace of the nation's burgeoning technology services industry gave a powerful boost to our economic partnership.

Since becoming India's prime minister in May 2014, Prime Minister Modi has surprised America's security community with his forward-leaning views on Asian security, which largely parallel our own. Our shared views were most significantly stated in the powerful "Joint Strategic Vision for the Asia Pacific and Indian Ocean Region," released during President Barack Obama's visit to India in January 2015. We have also made progress on our long-stalled "Defense Technology and Trade Initiative (DTTI)" programs for co-development and co-production of defense materiel, as well as renewing our defense framework agreement for another ten years. India has become one of the largest markets for U.S. defense exports, and a major partner for joint exercises; we also worked together effectively in our relief efforts following Nepal's devastating earthquake in April 2015.

Our economic relationship, however, is not yet guided by shared principles, at least at the policy level. Our attempts to negotiate a bilateral investment treaty have scarcely progressed since the day President Obama took office. The Modi government delayed its commitment to adopt the World Trade Organization's Trade Facilitation Agreement in mid-2014. India remains outside of regional and sectoral trade agreements that could have otherwise brought our two nations closer together, such as the Trade in Services Agreement and the expansion of the Information

Technology Agreement. And economic policymaking in India involves equal parts liberalization, protectionism, and ambiguity.

Of course, government-to-government engagement is only one leg of our economic partnership—and not the most important. American businesses themselves have shown renewed interest in India since the start of the Modi government. India has pulled in around $40 billion in foreign direct investment in the 12 months up to January 2016, a 20 percent increase on the prior year, and our bilateral trade relationship has remained steady despite a global slowdown in trade flows. This is due to a mixture of real reform, expected reform, and India's relative outperformance of other large economies.

Business associations and other commentators regularly lament that they expected more, deeper reforms by this point, but the Modi government's track record is solid, if unspectacular. Some highlights include:
- Easing foreign equity restrictions on over thirty sectors.
- Opening the coal sector to full private sector participation.
- Dramatically liberalizing the oil and gas exploration and marketing industry.
- Holding transparent auctions for public goods such as mining leases and telecommunications spectrum.
- Clamping down, though imperfectly, on instances of harassment of foreign investors by tax authorities.
- Creating an environment where state leaders more eagerly compete with each other to strengthen their business environments.

This last point, on the state business environment, is worth discussing in more depth. While most of our metrics for judging India's business environment is based on actions by the central government, state governments actually play a far more important role for most industries. State governments control factors such as electricity availability, water distribution, sanitation, law and order, land acquisition, and more. Most licenses required to establish and maintain a business are granted by state governments.

Which leads to an important point for this Subcommittee's consideration—the need to create a strong, coherent strategy to engage India's powerful state leaders. The BJP today, despite holding a majority of seats in the lower house of India's Parliament, only controls 8 of India's 29 states. India's other national party, the Congress Party, holds another 8 states. Regional parties control the rest. In fact, there are only seven states in India that have NOT been controlled by a regional party at some point since 2000- Chhattisgarh, Gujarat, Himachal Pradesh, Madhya Pradesh, Maharashtra, Rajasthan, and Uttarakhand.

Apart from shaping the local business environments across India, these regional parties also comprise a significant share of members of Parliament—particularly, today, in the upper house (Rajya Sabha), where the Congress and BJP combined only hold 47 percent of the total seats. So when difficult votes take place that matter to the United States—such as the recent decision to liberalize the foreign equity restriction in insurance, the trust vote over the civilian nuclear agreement in 2008, or the 2011 vote on India's civilian nuclear liability regime—these regional parties can have decisive influence. Yet for many regional leaders, the concept of cooperation with the United States does not hold much meaning, beyond a basic desire for American corporate investment. I believe that by engaging these state leaders more effectively, we can widen the overall base of support for our bilateral engagement—particularly on economic issues.

A more cogent example of the need to thoughtfully engage India's states is in clean energy. Clean energy has been at the forefront of U.S. foreign policy in recent years, and we have often articulated our desire for India to adopt cleaner forms of electric power generation as part of its energy mix going forward. While we put our hopes on Prime Minister Modi and his cabinet as our interlocutors, in fact, under India's constitution, electricity is a state subject. Most forms of renewable power remain more expensive than their fossil fuel equivalents, and India's state electricity utilities tend to be in poor financial and operational shape, due to a range of factors. State governments will be naturally inclined to look to low cost fuels for additional electric power generation. The central government does have tools to encourage states to make choices in this regard, but if we really want to see progress, the most important decisions in India's electric power sector will ultimately be up to twenty-nine leaders, not one.

The importance of state leaders and regional parties is not in question. Our nation's economic engagement strategy with India must take this into account, and result in constructive actions. Not every state leader will be receptive to outreach, but many will. This engagement can open up new export opportunities, new contracting opportunities, and new investment opportunities for American firms. And this boost to our overall economic engagement will help cement our growing partnership.

Overall, America's relationship with India has prospered fairly rapidly in the last twenty years. And we have seen a quickening of this growth in the last two years. But our two countries have made far more progress, at the policy level, in establishing a set of shared security principles, while we still focus our economic engagement on a series of modest goals without a strong ideological underpinning. Our leaders must redouble efforts to find common ideological ground on economic issues, or risk suffering quick downturns in the relationship as we did in late 2013. And a core facet of American economic engagement going forward must focus on India's powerful regional leaders—both for their outsize role in truly shaping India's business environment, and also for their powerful role in shaping India's national policies.

Mr. SALMON. Thank you very much.

I think the reason that nobody gets to be Secretary of State based on their policy on India is they are not big enough troublemakers. So, I guess we ought to be thankful for that.

My two questions center on foreign direct investment. First of all, Prime Minister Modi recently launched efforts to boost India's domestic manufacturing base and promote economic growth from within with programs like Make in India Campaign. Does the Make in India Campaign program discriminate against U.S. and foreign manufacturers and imports? Will this policy hinder foreign direct investment? Do you think that it will have an adverse effect maybe on securing the kind of foreign investment it needs?

Then, secondly, related to their existing foreign direct investment policy which prohibits foreign-owned businesses from selling items directly to the Indian consumers over the internet, should that policy be one that Modi looks at reforming? Is that going to hurt foreign direct investment as well?

So, Mr. Rossow, do you want to take a stab first?

Mr. ROSSOW. Yes. Let me start with the second one on sales via the internet. I am actually working on a piece right now to try to break down the various and strange ways that companies have to contort in order to sell something to a consumer in India.

So, if you are selling to businesses, there is one regulatory regime. You know that, yes, broken down. They have already started to liberalize on e-commerce to some extent.

The idea about marketplace, kind of like eBay, where individuals sell to individuals via an administered platform, that is already allowed. Or just say that it is not discriminated against. So, that is one model that is allowed.

If you manufacture in India, you are allowed to sell online directly to consumers. And if you have single-brand investment in India, so like a Nike store or Apple store, you are allowed to sell directly to consumers.

Those changes have been made largely under the Modi government so far. So, they have incrementally, I think, been chipping away at the ban on foreign investment in e-commerce. But, still, the big opening I think on a multi-brand, you know, the kind of e-commerce platforms that we see here in the United States where you buy directly from businesses carrying multiple brands over the internet still isn't there.

Now my conversations with Indian officials, it is on the cusp. I suspect that is one of the reforms I think in the next year or two you are going to see. They have been, as I mentioned, kind of incrementally moving their way in that direction. So, I think it is on, I would say, the short list of next FDI reforms. But, as to the timing, is it 6 months from now or a year from now, I can't be sure.

Mr. SALMON. Do you think that it could be a substantial left reform? So, a company like let's say Amazon could actually sell directly to consumers? Do you think that it might liberalize that much?

Mr. ROSSOW. Yes, I think it might. But what you have to watch out for is are there going to be provisions on local sourcing rules, things like that that in other areas where they have opened up retail trade have proved to be a bit of a poison pill. So, you always look for what are the qualifiers that will attach to a policy like that. Some policies get opened up to 100-percent foreign investment with very few restrictions. Other policies you see things in there that would actually preclude investors coming in.

Amazon, though, is actually one of the largest e-retailers in India right now, but it is on the marketplace model.

Mr. SALMON. Right. It is on a marketplace model and, otherwise, they can sell to businesses, but they can't sell directly to consumers.

Mr. ROSSOW. Yes, it is a strange tree, watching the different ways you try to get something in consumers' hands.

Mr. SALMON. What about the other question? And, Dr. Ayres, you could address it or Mr. Dhume, whoever feels more adequate. But the Make in India policy, does that have the potential to discriminate against foreign manufacturers, foreign investors? Is that something we should be maybe chatting with them about?

Ms. AYRES. I think, first of all, having the platform of Make in India is, first and foremost, designed to attract foreign direct investment into India. A lot of American companies that are manufacturing in India are taking advantage of that. So, it is actually helpful to the larger revenue of some American companies.

For example, General Motors announced $1-billion investment and a relocation of a factory last summer. Ford has one of their largest manufacturing facilities anywhere in the world in Gujarat. There is a long list of others.

Since the Make in India initiative was announced in September 2014, there has been a trickle of major investment announcements. And so, I think we would have to look at kind of individual sectors to see if there was anything that would preclude or prohibit or limit U.S. exports to India. So, I don't think it is possible to answer that in a blanket, kind of umbrella statement.

But, certainly, it is the case that this is a platform that is helpful to some American manufacturers who are looking to produce for this huge and growing Indian market.

Mr. DHUME. Let me take a quick stab at both of those. On the e-commerce, I would agree with what Rick said. It is important to keep in perspective that India's e-commerce market is one of the most interesting and one of the fastest-growing in the world. There was a statistic recently I saw which said that the top three e-commerce sites in India do more business than the top ten offline retailers combined. One of those top three is Amazon.

Mr. SALMON. Okay.

Mr. DHUME. So, it is definitely there. It is a player. There is certainly room for further reform over there. I agree that it is probably coming down the pike, but the situation now, it is already we do have—there is a stake.

On Make in India, I think your question, it is a very important question because there is a philosophical difference and there is a difference between a Make in India which says we are going to make India a more attractive place to do business and a Make in India that says we are going to make it hard to do business unless you make in India.

Mr. SALMON. Right.

Mr. DHUME. I think that is what the question is driving at. I would say that, so far, the emphasis of the government has been on the former, but it is certainly something that we should continue to watch and continue to pay attention to. But, if you look at FDI over the last 20 months, the first 20 months of the Modi government, FDI in India has risen by 33 percent.

Mr. SALMON. Right.

Mr. DHUME. So, it has definitely been very foreign-investment-friendly.

Mr. SALMON. Thanks, Mr. Dhume.

Mr. Sherman?

Mr. SHERMAN. Thank you.

In evaluating trade relationships, we all too often focus on revenue for American corporations or profits for American corporations, and all too little emphasis is put on jobs for American workers.

I would point out that Japan runs a $5-billion surplus or a $4-billion to $5-billion surplus with India. Germany runs a $5-billion surplus with India. There are two possible explanations of why we are running a deficit. One is that our workers are not as good. The other is that our Government is not as good at representing the interests of American workers. I think that the elites in Washington should plead guilty because it is the second and not the first.

Mr. Rossow, what changes in U.S. law, policy, or regulation is India seeking?

Mr. ROSSOW. Changes on this side, that is a great question, rarely asked, I think, in our bilateral relationship. They want more visas. They want lower visa fees. They would like a Social Security agreement that allows Social Security payments made by H-1B-holders to be exempted from payment or reimbursed at the other end. So, they do have, I think, a short number of issues.

Mr. SHERMAN. So, all of those things relate to how immigrants and/or diaspora workers are treated. Anything on trade?

Mr. ROSSOW. On trade, there are still some technology——

Mr. SHERMAN. Investment? Any of the things that we usually negotiate? Anything that our Trade Representative's Office would actually deal with?

Mr. ROSSOW. Right now, we are looking at an investment treaty as probably the biggest thing that is on the agenda.

Mr. SHERMAN. Yes, it is on the agenda, but is there anything that India is seeking in that investment treaty or are they just kind of talking to us because it is one of the things we like to talk about?

Mr. ROSSOW. Yes, every meeting I have with Indian Government officials, they have a difficult time articulating what is kind of in it for them, because they have got access to our market. So, it is really is, will that be attractive enough to bring new investors to India in the sectors they desire, rather than it being a market access opportunity for Indian firms on our side.

Mr. SHERMAN. And that investment may deprive Americans of work. Indians watch a lot of movies. A lot of movies are made in India. What are the restrictions on American firms, Hollywood, having their movies exhibited on screens and TV sets in India? Mr. Rossow?

Mr. Rossow. I am not aware of any restrictions based on American movies being there. There are some restrictions on TV channels, foreign ownership of TV channels and things like that, which could be a pipeline for more American contents coming into India, but, otherwise, unrestricted.

Mr. Sherman. Is any of the other witnesses aware?

Mr. Dhume. I was just in India last week and I watched The Revenant with my parents, and they absolutely loved that bear scene. So, a lot of Hollywood movies in India.

Mr. Sherman. Yes, there are a lot of Hollywood movies in China, but they restrict us to 30 or 40 movies. There are no similar restrictions in India?

Mr. Dhume. Netflix has just come to India also, and I expect it to do quite well. It is a large market.

Mr. Sherman. What are the primary barriers to U.S. companies exporting goods and services to India? Mr. Rossow?

Mr. Rossow. Well, there still are a number of sectors where they have put up restrictions on foreign companies selling in the market. So, for instance, let's talk about defense trade. There is a 30-percent direct offset requirement for defense sales. You have to produce some portion of that locally.

The solar policy, which demands local content to qualify for certain tax benefits, there were policies developed during the last government, which this government hasn't removed, which look at local content as well for government contracts on electronics, on communications, things like that.

So, there are a wide range of sectors where there are, I think, more explicit rules that limit American trade or force some of it under local content to be able to qualify for certain deals. Those are the main ones that I am aware of.

Mr. Sherman. India will be building nuclear power plants. We in Congress stepped forward and approved the Nuclear Cooperation Agreement. The thinking in India is that there will be some plants built by the United States. But, as a practical matter, Russian and French firms are government-owned and, therefore, they have sovereign immunity and could never be sued; whereas, a U.S. firm could be. We have turned to other countries to have liability protection, which really just puts our companies in the same position as the French and Russian companies. Obviously, Bhopal is still remembered in India.

We voted for the U.S.-India Energy Cooperation Agreement. Are we going to get any jobs out of it? Mr. Rossow?

Mr. Rossow. I think we will. I mean, talks about actually creating a liability regime in India that will accommodate American interests for developing are ongoing. American companies aren't allowed to actually invest in the plants there. So, it is going to be contracts as suppliers. Will the material be built in India? Probably not anytime soon for American companies. So, I think so, but it depends upon whether or not they get this workaround for the liability issue done in a way that accommodates American trading concerns. So, it looks like it is headed in the right direction, but nothing is done.

Mr. Sherman. I will ask one other question.

Mr. Dhume. Can I just add?

Mr. SHERMAN. Yes.

Mr. DHUME. I will just add to that very briefly. I think that it is a completely valid concern. I think that there is reason to be concerned that this has taken so long and that, despite many years after the agreement, there hasn't been concrete——

Mr. SHERMAN. Is it well understood in India that they are, in effect, providing liability insulation for the French and Russian companies?

Mr. DHUME. I think it is viewed, as you alluded to in your question, mostly through the prism of Bhopal, which is why you had that liability law passed in 2010 which was very tough.

But I think there is something that we sometimes lose sight of when we are discussing the nuclear issue, which is that, though there may not have been sufficient progress on that particular issue, the nuclear deal really has unlocked the relationship in many other ways.

Mr. SHERMAN. Thank you for that. I am going to try to sneak in one more question with a two-word answer from each witness.

Pick two states in India where you think it is easiest for Americans to do business.

Mr. DHUME. Gujarat and Andhra Pradesh, I would say.

Mr. ROSSOW. Yes, Andhra Pradesh. I will say Maharashtra, just to be a little bit different.

Mr. SHERMAN. Is Gujarat one of your two or——

Mr. ROSSOW. I probably would pick that. If you would give me three, I would say those three, Maharashtra, Gujarat, and Andhra.

Mr. SHERMAN. And Dr. Ayres?

Ms. AYRES. I agree. I would say either of those three.

Mr. SHERMAN. Okay. We have got three instead of two.

I yield back.

Mr. SALMON. I turn to Mr. Chabot. But, before you get to ask the witnesses questions, we are all kind of wanting to know from you who is going to win in Ohio tonight. [Laughter.]

Mr. CHABOT. I have no idea.

Mr. SALMON. Mr. Chabot?

Mr. CHABOT. Thank you. Thank you, Mr. Chairman, for holding this important hearing.

Many consider the U.S.-India relationship an indispensable one, and I tend to believe that myself. India is already a regional economic powerhouse and could potentially become one of the most important powers in the world. I think the U.S. has, for the most part, succeeded in fostering this relationship over the years.

For more than a decade, the U.S. has committed to working with India to ensure a lasting strategic relationship. Both countries identify our bilateral trade ties as an integral component to our relationship moving forward.

I would stress, as I have in past hearings on this topic—I chaired this committee in the previous Session of Congress, not Session of Congress, but previous Congress—that it is essential for the administration to continue proactive engagement with India. Many of us in Congress and in the administration welcomed Prime Minister Modi's ascension to power with pretty significant enthusiasm.

Now, however, I am beginning to hear skepticism about the Modi government's follow-through in some areas; for example, its commitment to promoting stronger economic relations. I am particularly concerned with India's commitment to respect intellectual property rights, and the administration should take the necessary steps to ensure that American innovations are afforded the safeguards that they deserve, and that our American businesses, particularly our small businesses—I happen to the chairman of the House Small Business Committee now—that our small businesses can rely upon this administration and the Federal Government to do everything it can to protect their interests. After all, if we want to continue to be the world leader in international trade, we must continue to prioritize these kinds of issues.

Now for a couple of questions. Last fall the International Trade Commission found that the Modi government had made no changes to its laws to address longstanding intellectual-property-related trade barriers. Moreover, India's long-awaited IPR policy is rumored to be far less of an improvement than hoped. Is India backsliding on these issues? What can we do to get India to create a level playing field for our exporters and our investors? I would be happy to hear from any of the panel members on this. Dr. Ayres?

Ms. AYRES. I will offer some initial thoughts on that.

First, I think in the IPR conversation we should probably split the discussion to talk first about copyright issues and, then, secondly, IPR concerns in other industries. The pharmaceutical industry in the United States has some deep concerns about India's IPR regime.

On the copyright side, there has actually been a lot of good news. That has been an arena where you have seen Indian industry, particularly India's media and entertainment industry, step up and request its state-level governments and its government at the Federal level to put in place stronger protections for copyright. So, that has actually happened, and I think you now have seen over the course of the last decade a real convergence of views in the entertainment space. So, whether it is songwriting or a script or a film, we have now, I think, got agreement with the regime in India on copyright.

IPR, as you referred to, is much more difficult. I don't believe that India is backsliding, but I don't believe that their patent law has moved in any way in a direction that would be satisfactory to what people in the United States are looking for.

I know that the Indian Government recently received an opinion from the World Trade Organization that supported India's patent law. So, I do not anticipate that that positive opinion they received from the WTO would suggest to Indian lawmakers a necessity for them changing their own law. What that tells me is I think we are going to continue to see a lot of fireworks over the IPR issues, particularly in the pharmaceutical industry, for the next several years. I don't see this as an issue that is going to be easily remedied.

Mr. CHABOT. Okay. Thank you.

Mr. Dhume?

Mr. DHUME. I would just add very quickly that I would share the characterization that there has been neither concrete forward movement nor visible backsliding. I think that on the positive side, some of the fears that people had 2 or 3 years ago about, for instance, compulsory licensing have not come to pass. Things have sort of been frozen in place. But it certainly does seem that the area of concern would probably be things like drug pricing where it is a very live political issue in terms of how much companies should charge. And that is the area that I would be paying the most attention to.

Mr. CHABOT. Thank you.

Mr. Chairman, my time has expired. Do we have time to hear from Mr. Rossow?

Mr. SALMON. Yes.

Mr. CHABOT. Thank you.

Yes, sir?

Mr. ROSSOW. I agree with, actually, what both said. Areas like development of film and content and things like that where India has an offensive interest, we have got a lot of alignment. But, on pharmaceutical, our industries are based on different models. And so, it is very difficult for us to kind of bridge that gap. It is absolutely night and day. So, to find common ground in that scenario is extremely difficult.

But Sadanand had mentioned on pharmaceutical pricing, it is kind of a new issue that we see, I think, new attempts to regulate pricing. Also, medical devices is another issue that is kind of like related to that that we are seeing. So, nothing further than what my colleagues had said on that.

Mr. CHABOT. Thank you.

I yield back.

Mr. SALMON. Thank you.

Mr. Lowenthal?

Mr. LOWENTHAL. Thank you, Mr. Chair.

I am going to follow up some of the questions I thought in terms of India's relationships to its neighbors per se. Can you tell us how it is improving trade or what its trade relationships are with Pakistan, with China, with Sri Lanka? Where is that moving? And maybe explain to us how India is dealing with its regional partners.

Ms. AYRES. Perhaps I will take a stab at that and, then, my colleagues might have some additional thoughts.

China is India's largest trading partner in goods. We have heard earlier the United States is India's largest trading partner in goods and services, but China is India's number one in goods. So, it has a very robust economic relationship with China.

India is not happy with the balance of its trade with China. India feels that it is sending out raw materials and importing finished goods. So, it is unhappy about the trade balance and the composition of trade.

Mr. LOWENTHAL. Yes.

Ms. AYRES. With Pakistan, India is in an extremely-limited trade relationship. In 1994 or 1996—I would have to check my notes—India granted Pakistan most favored nation recognition. Pakistan has never reciprocated that. So, they don't have free and open trade.

There have been some studies done that suggest that they have got trade diversion that goes through the Gulf, through the United Arab Emirates, instead of going across the border by land, where it could be carried out quite easily.

Previous Indian Governments and the Indian and Pakistani private sector have tried to use trade initiatives to try to be a kind of leading edge to improve ties. But, without that most favored nation recognition and some sort of larger push on trade, it is hard to see larger improvement on the trade ties.

With the smaller countries around India, there is an open border with Nepal. So, they have free and open trade and movement of persons anyway. India has a free trade agreement with Sri Lanka that has expanded their trading relationship significantly. And India recently completed a boundary reorganization with Bangladesh, and they have significantly expanded the trade with Bangladesh. So, economic ties with Bangladesh have been a big focus for the Indian Government.

Mr. DHUME. I agree with all of that. I would just say that, if you were to look at India and you look around, basically, with all the smaller countries, trade relations have been improving, deepening. Barriers have been lowered.

The two problems are China and Pakistan, for different reasons. The India-China relationship in some ways is like the U.S.-China relationship in terms of trade. It is lopsided. India has market access issues. Nonetheless, it is a very large economic partners.

With Pakistan, it is really a question of access. The key over there is that India would like to see trade dealt with as a separate issue and trade to be pursued; whereas, Pakistan would like trade to be linked to other issues, such as security, and that has been a sticking point.

Mr. ROSSOW. I will just tie in a loop your question and the chairman's question, actually. The sectors that I mentioned where India has restrictions on foreign trade, whether it is solar, electronics, IT, telecom equipment, this is pretty much China's top exports to India.

So, when these issues came up, it wasn't reaction because, of course, we have a trade deficit. It is exactly not explicitly, but going after the areas where China has major exports to India.

India's trade balance overall is declining in the last couple of years, as a lot of countries are, but their trade deficit with China continues to go up. So, that has even been augmented while they have been reducing oil imports and other things as prices come down.

Mr. LOWENTHAL. Thank you.

I just have one other question. You have all touched on it. I think, Dr. Ayres, you talked about it also, about some of the legal protections, or lack thereof, in India. I am just wondering, is the legal system or the rule of law attractive enough for foreign investment into India now? Do companies believe that they have the kinds of legal protections that they need? Anyone?

Mr. DHUME. I think large companies do. Large companies that have the resources when cases come up to prosecute it effectively, hire the best law firms, get it through the appeals process to higher courts, where you know you are going to get a very good hearing, they have managed to do fairly well. Some major cases involving some of the biggest investors in the country, recently Vodafone, a few years before that Morgan Stanley with a big tax case, they managed to get those all the way to the Supreme Court of India in just a couple of years.

But the small and medium businesses I think, for them, where maybe they don't have the kind of resources to put toward the case, they would have to churn it out, just like Indian companies would. That sometimes can take several years to get through.

So, I think it moves fast enough and it is fair for large companies with the resources to spend the time and energy to do it. Small and medium companies, I think they continue to be concerned about this. So, I will leave it at that.

Mr. DHUME. I mean, I think you could divide that into a bird's eye view and a worm's eye view. From a bird's eye view, it looks great, the British legal system, rule of law, and all of that. From the worm's eye view, for firms it often depends from case to case and it can be messy and time-consuming.

But, by and large, if you sort of look at India and compare it to most of the developing world in Asia, I would say that rule of law is generally seen as one of the positive attributes of India.

Mr. LOWENTHAL. Thank you.

And I yield back.

Mr. SALMON. Thank you.

Ms. Gabbard?

Ms. GABBARD. Thank you, Mr. Chairman.

Aloha. Welcome.

Since 2008, the U.S. and India have signed more than $10 billion in defense contracts, and the Defense Trade and Technology Initiative has been a priority in these bilateral security relations. Especially now with Secretary Carter as our Secretary of Defense, I think this has continued to be a priority.

Can you speak to your assessment of how the DTTI is working and, if there are impediments, what are they and how can they be overcome?

Ms. AYRES. So, I will offer a couple of thoughts. I know my fellow panelists have been thinking about this one as well.

The DTTI seems to be going very well. As with almost everything involving negotiating some sort of agreement with India, it is not happening overnight, and I don't think that should surprise us. But the fact that we have seen an increase, first, in the defense procurements, which is good for our economy as well as good for India's developing its defense and security capacity; the fact that we now have these pathfinder projects that are moving ahead; the fact that we have seen a change in India's FDI policy when it comes to the defense sector, moving that FDI cap from 26 to 49 percent, with the possibility of up to 100 percent on a case-by-case basis, these are all positive movements that have been helpful to the defense industry. I would anticipate that as discussion of the projects, the pathfinder projects, continues, we will come together and be able to produce something and develop something with India. So, I consider that moving quite positively.

Ms. GABBARD. Okay. Before you respond, I will just add to the question about these three foundational agreements that I hear from Admiral Harry Harris and others frequently about being so critical to enhancing U.S.-India partnerships and their hope that India will sign those foundational agreements. If you could add that to your response of where you think that is at and if they will sign?

Mr. DHUME. On DTTI, I would add one other sort of broader reason for optimism is the Make in India policy that was mentioned earlier and, also, raising foreign investment caps in India in the defense sector. So, there is genuine optimism that there will be more U.S. investment and genuine partnership over there, including in defense manufacturing, and there is certainly a lot of interest in that in India.

On the logistical agreements, I don't know what the latest on that is, but my understanding is that, with the new Defense Minister Parrikar, there is greater interest in India going ahead and signing those agreements than we had in the previous administration.

Ms. GABBARD. Thank you.

Mr. ROSSOW. I think the previous administration and the fact that they had such strong support from the communist parties in India, they managed to tilt the discussions over the foundation agreements, so that it sounded like India was giving away the store, that a logistical sharing agreement meant that we had open basing with India, that we had backdoor channels where we can steal communications from the equipment we sold.

The fact that the communists are no longer a force, the BJP is not reliant upon them, that voice I think that managed to sink it last time around, when those talks began 8 years ago, is gone. So, that leaves an open door.

I mean, it is in the press right now that these talks are happening. You don't feel that kind of blowback against it. So, I think the stage is set for progress on the foundation agreements.

On the Defense Technology and Trade Initiative, I think that exactly exhibits why long-term vision is critical, because we have put forward more than a dozen projects to the Indian side and got no response. But, as soon as we started talking about aircraft carrier technology, jet engines, the things that hit exactly on where India saw its future and strategic interests, as soon as we put those on the table as longer-term working groups, they came back and we got four project agreements, well, we got four agreements and, then, two which will result in project agreements. So, we have only got four. Two of those don't look like they are moving very fast. Hopefully, we can get some new ones added to the list now.

But I see tremendous progress. Even if there frustration occasionally that two of them aren't moving that quickly, it is talked about as one of the most tangible, cogent examples about where partnership goes. So, in terms of a guiding star, I think it has also provided a great opportunity for us.

Ms. GABBARD. Yes. Great. Thank you very much.

Thank you, Mr. Chairman.

Mr. SALMON. I would like to really thank the panelists for giving us the opportunity today to learn more about the bilateral opportunities that exist, predominantly in the trade opportunities, but others as well.

It is clear that India is moving in leaps and bounds and that, regardless of how these hearings turn out, they are going to continue to progress. We need to figure out how to better partner with them on different ideas because I think their success globally as well as success in the region can be enhanced by a strong U.S.-India relationship. I, for one, am really hopeful that we can move forward with a Bilateral Investment Treaty. I think that would be incredibly positive.

There are other things that we have heard expressed, that the lawsuits tend to take a long, long time, on the average I think 4 years, to get resolved. While big companies have the resources to stay the course, that becomes difficult. And with the pharmaceutical companies, the generic entry into the markets has been a concern.

But, as we move forward, I think that most of the issues are very resolvable between our countries. I would echo what Mr. Bera said. When we were able to go to India, we were afforded great courtesies as far as opportunity to meet with Prime Minister Modi and virtually all of his Cabinet for several hours. It showed me that they are keenly interested in strengthening the relationships with us. And so, I think that is a real positive thing.

I would like to really thank the panelists for coming today.

I would like to thank the ranking member.

Mr. SHERMAN. May I join you in those comments?

Mr. SALMON. Yes, yes.

Mr. SHERMAN. I want to thank the panel for coming here, and I look forward to the U.S.-India relationship not being our 10th largest trading partner in the future.

Mr. SALMON. Absolutely, and let's do a better job. I do echo what Mr. Sherman says. Let's start doing a better job in getting our products over there. China has really taken great advantage of us when it comes to that lopsided agreement, and we don't want to make the same mistakes with India.

But thank you very much for being here today.

This committee is now adjourned.

[Whereupon, at 3:26 p.m., the subcommittee was adjourned.]

APPENDIX

SUBCOMMITTEE HEARING NOTICE
COMMITTEE ON FOREIGN AFFAIRS
U.S. HOUSE OF REPRESENTATIVES
WASHINGTON, DC 20515-6128

Subcommittee on Asia and the Pacific
Matt Salmon (R-AZ), Chairman

March 15, 2016

TO: MEMBERS OF THE COMMITTEE ON FOREIGN AFFAIRS

You are respectfully requested to attend an OPEN hearing of the Committee on Foreign Affairs, to be held by the Subcommittee on Asia and the Pacific in Room 2172 of the Rayburn House Office Building (and available live on the Committee website at http://www.ForeignAffairs.house.gov):

DATE: Tuesday, March 15, 2016

TIME: 2:00 p.m.

SUBJECT: U.S.-India Relations: Democratic Partners of Economic Opportunity

WITNESSES: Alyssa Ayres, Ph.D.
Senior Fellow for India, Pakistan, and South Asia
Council on Foreign Relations

Mr. Sadanand Dhume
Resident Fellow
American Enterprise Institute

Mr. Richard M. Rossow
Senior Fellow and Wadhwani Chair in U.S.-India Policy Studies
Center for Strategic and International Studies

**NOTE: Further witnesses may be added.

By Direction of the Chairman

The Committee on Foreign Affairs seeks to make its facilities accessible to persons with disabilities. If you are in need of special accommodations, please call 202/225-5021 at least four business days in advance of the event, whenever practicable. Questions with regard to special accommodations in general (including availability of Committee materials in alternative formats and assistive listening devices) may be directed to the Committee.

COMMITTEE ON FOREIGN AFFAIRS

MINUTES OF SUBCOMMITTEE ON _____ *Asia and the Pacific* _____ HEARING

Day___*Tuesday*___Date_____*3/15/16*_____Room_____*2172*_____

Starting Time ____*2:20pm*____ Ending Time ___*3:25pm*___

Recesses |____| (____to ____) (____to ____) (____to ____) (____to ____) (____to ____) (____to ____)

Presiding Member(s)

Salmon

Check all of the following that apply:

Open Session ☑
Executive (closed) Session ☐
Televised ☐

Electronically Recorded (taped) ☐
Stenographic Record ☐

TITLE OF HEARING:

U.S.-India Relations: Democratic Partners of Economic Opportunity

SUBCOMMITTEE MEMBERS PRESENT:

Chabot
Sherman, Meng, Gabbard, Bera, Lowenthal

NON-SUBCOMMITTEE MEMBERS PRESENT: *(Mark with an * if they are not members of full committee.)*

HEARING WITNESSES: Same as meeting notice attached? Yes ☑ **No** ☐
(If "no", please list below and include title, agency, department, or organization.)

STATEMENTS FOR THE RECORD: *(List any statements submitted for the record.)*

TIME SCHEDULED TO RECONVENE _____
or
TIME ADJOURNED ____*3:25*____

Subcommittee Staff Director

MATERIAL SUBMITTED FOR THE RECORD BY ALYSSA AYRES, PH.D., SENIOR FELLOW FOR INDIA, PAKISTAN, AND SOUTH ASIA, COUNCIL ON FOREIGN RELATIONS

COUNCIL *on* FOREIGN RELATIONS

Independent Task Force Report No. 73

Charles R. Kaye and Joseph S. Nye Jr., *Chairs*
Alyssa Ayres, *Project Director*

Working With a Rising India

A Joint Venture for the New Century

COUNCIL *on*
FOREIGN
RELATIONS

Independent Task Force Report No. 73

Charles R. Kaye and
Joseph S. Nye Jr., *Chairs*
Alyssa Ayres, *Project Director*

Working With a Rising India
A Joint Venture for the New Century

The Council on Foreign Relations (CFR) is an independent, nonpartisan membership organization, think tank, and publisher dedicated to being a resource for its members, government officials, business executives, journalists, educators and students, civic and religious leaders, and other interested citizens in order to help them better understand the world and the foreign policy choices facing the United States and other countries. Founded in 1921, CFR carries out its mission by maintaining a diverse membership, with special programs to promote interest and develop expertise in the next generation of foreign policy leaders; convening meetings at its headquarters in New York and in Washington, DC, and other cities where senior government officials, members of Congress, global leaders, and prominent thinkers come together with CFR members to discuss and debate major international issues; supporting a Studies Program that fosters independent research, enabling CFR scholars to produce articles, reports, and books and hold roundtables that analyze foreign policy issues and make concrete policy recommendations; publishing *Foreign Affairs*, the preeminent journal on international affairs and U.S. foreign policy; sponsoring Independent Task Forces that produce reports with both findings and policy prescriptions on the most important foreign policy topics; and providing up-to-date information and analysis about world events and American foreign policy on its website, www.cfr.org.

The Council on Foreign Relations takes no institutional positions on policy issues and has no affiliation with the U.S. government. All views expressed in its publications and on its website are the sole responsibility of the author or authors.

The Council on Foreign Relations sponsors Independent Task Forces to assess issues of current and critical importance to U.S. foreign policy and provide policymakers with concrete judgments and recommendations. Diverse in backgrounds and perspectives, Task Force members aim to reach a meaningful consensus on policy through private deliberations. Once launched, Task Forces are independent of CFR and solely responsible for the content of their reports. Task Force members are asked to join a consensus signifying that they endorse "the general policy thrust and judgments reached by the group, though not necessarily every finding and recommendation." Each Task Force member also has the option of putting forward an additional or dissenting view. Members' affiliations are listed for identification purposes only and do not imply institutional endorsement. Task Force observers participate in discussions, but are not asked to join the consensus.

For further information about CFR or this Task Force, please write to the Council on Foreign Relations, 58 East 68th Street, New York, NY 10065, or call the Communications office at 212.434.9888. Visit CFR's website at www.cfr.org.

Task Force Members

Task Force members are asked to join a consensus signifying that they endorse "the general policy thrust and judgments reached by the group, though not necessarily every finding and recommendation." They participate in the Task Force in their individual, not institutional, capacities.

Alyssa Ayres*
Council on Foreign Relations

Ajay Banga*
MasterCard

C. Fred Bergsten
Peterson Institute for International Economics

Marshall M. Bouton*
Chicago Council on Global Affairs

Nicholas Burns
Harvard University

Stephen P. Cohen*
Brookings Institution

Richard Fontaine
Center for a New American Security

Sumit Ganguly*
Indiana University, Bloomington

Helene D. Gayle
McKinsey Social Initiative

Charles R. Kaye
Warburg Pincus LLC

Mary Kissel*
Wall Street Journal

Joseph S. Nye Jr.
Harvard University

Gary Roughead
Hoover Institution

Mariko Silver
Bennington College

Ashley J. Tellis*
Carnegie Endowment for International Peace

Member, ex officio
Robert D. Blackwill
Council on Foreign Relations

*The individual has endorsed the report and signed an additional view.

Contents

Foreword ix
Acknowledgments xiii
Acronyms xvii

Independent Task Force Report 1
Executive Summary 3
Introduction 9
Background 13
U.S.-India Relations: A Reformulation for the Future 25
Priorities for the Joint-Venture Future 32
Conclusion 47

Additional Views 49
Endnotes 52
Task Force Members 55
Task Force Observers 64

Foreword

Eighteen years ago, I chaired a Council on Foreign Relations–sponsored Independent Task Force on South Asia, *A New U.S. Policy Toward India and Pakistan*, which was followed up by a second Task Force report one year later after both India and Pakistan tested nuclear weapons. Rereading those reports serves to remind how two decades ago nonproliferation was the dominant lens through which Washington viewed its interests in India and South Asia. Today, with the end of the Cold War, the emergence of terrorism with a global reach, a long war in Afghanistan, the rise of China, and India's economic growth, there is the reality of a much wider aperture.

U.S. relations with India have changed as well. Bilateral ties are closer than ever, including on sensitive strategic matters. India conducts more military exercises with the United States than with any other country, and increasingly, New Delhi and Washington confer on a wide range of issues, including global health, cybersecurity, clean energy, and democracy promotion. Prime Minister Narendra Modi has given special emphasis to India's ties with the United States, having just completed his second visit to this country, and having welcomed President Barack Obama to India's Republic Day parade, a first for a sitting U.S. president. Prime Minister Modi has made economics the cornerstone of his foreign policy, and has stated his goals of achieving faster economic growth and reducing the hurdles to doing business in India.

That said, many of the issues that previously limited the U.S. relationship with India remain, albeit to a lesser degree. While Washington and New Delhi have converged more closely on Asia-Pacific strategic matters and counterterrorism, Indian leaders do not always see Washington's global policy goals as congruent with their interests, especially regarding Iran and the Middle East. Indian policymakers also remain ambivalent about the market-based, open competition that has potential to power their economy and expand the U.S.-India economic relationship.

In some ways, it is possible to speak of two Indias—one of great accomplishment and promise, another that never quite lives up to its potential. It is similarly possible to speak of two U.S.-India relationships, one that broadens and deepens, another marked more by mutual disappointment and frustration. It is against this backdrop that the Council on Foreign Relations launched this Task Force—the first to focus exclusively on India—to assess the current situation in India and the U.S.-India relationship, and to develop findings and recommendations for U.S. foreign policy.

This report urges U.S. policymakers to reframe the terms they use in crafting a partnership with a rising India that does not seek an alliance relationship with the United States. It recommends seeing U.S.-India ties more as a joint venture. This term has specific meaning. As in business, joint ventures do not presuppose agreement on every matter outside those objectives. Narrowing and managing those inevitable differences will be critical to the U.S.-India relationship.

The Task Force offers a limited, prioritized set of additional recommendations. Among the most important for U.S. policymakers is the call to support India's economic growth. Making this the top priority for U.S.-India relations will require the United States to rethink its economic approach to India. The report offers steps to do so, including supporting Indian membership in the Asia-Pacific Economic Cooperation forum, completing a bilateral investment treaty, starting high-level discussion of bilateral sectoral agreements, crafting a long-term pathway to a free trade agreement or Indian membership in the Trans-Pacific Partnership, and further increasing defense trade.

The Task Force also urges Indian leaders to deepen their country's economic liberalization, something essential if India is to achieve sustained high growth rates. On strategic matters, the Task Force commends the recent expansion of defense ties, and urges renewed attention to homeland security and counterterrorism cooperation. Looking at the region, the Task Force recognizes the challenge to U.S.-India relations posed by U.S. policy toward Pakistan, as well as the drag on India's rise presented by the risk of conflict with Pakistan. The Task Force recommends that India—for the sake of its own future—pursue an improved relationship with Pakistan. In parallel, the Task Force urges the United States to demand that Pakistan tackle terrorism, and prepare to cease U.S. funding for defense sales and coalition support funds should Pakistan prove unwilling. The report also makes recommendations about priorities for collaboration on global issues, recognizing the cyber domain and global health as those with the greatest potential.

I would like to thank the Task Force's co-chairs, Charles R. "Chip" Kaye and Joseph S. Nye Jr., for their thoughtfulness, expert guidance, and commitment to producing a report that would result in real action by policymakers in both countries. I also thank the accomplished group of Task Force members and observers whose insights and knowledge contributed so much to the final product.

I am grateful to Chris Tuttle, managing director of CFR's Independent Task Force Program. His steady hand has been instrumental to the Task Force process. I would finally like to thank Project Director and Senior Fellow for India, Pakistan, and South Asia Alyssa Ayres for helping to guide the deliberations and drafting the important report that they produced.

Richard N. Haass
President
Council on Foreign Relations
November 2015

[NOTE: The above document is not reprinted here in its entirety but may be found at: http://docs.house.gov/Committee/Calendar/ByEvent.aspx?EventID=104671]